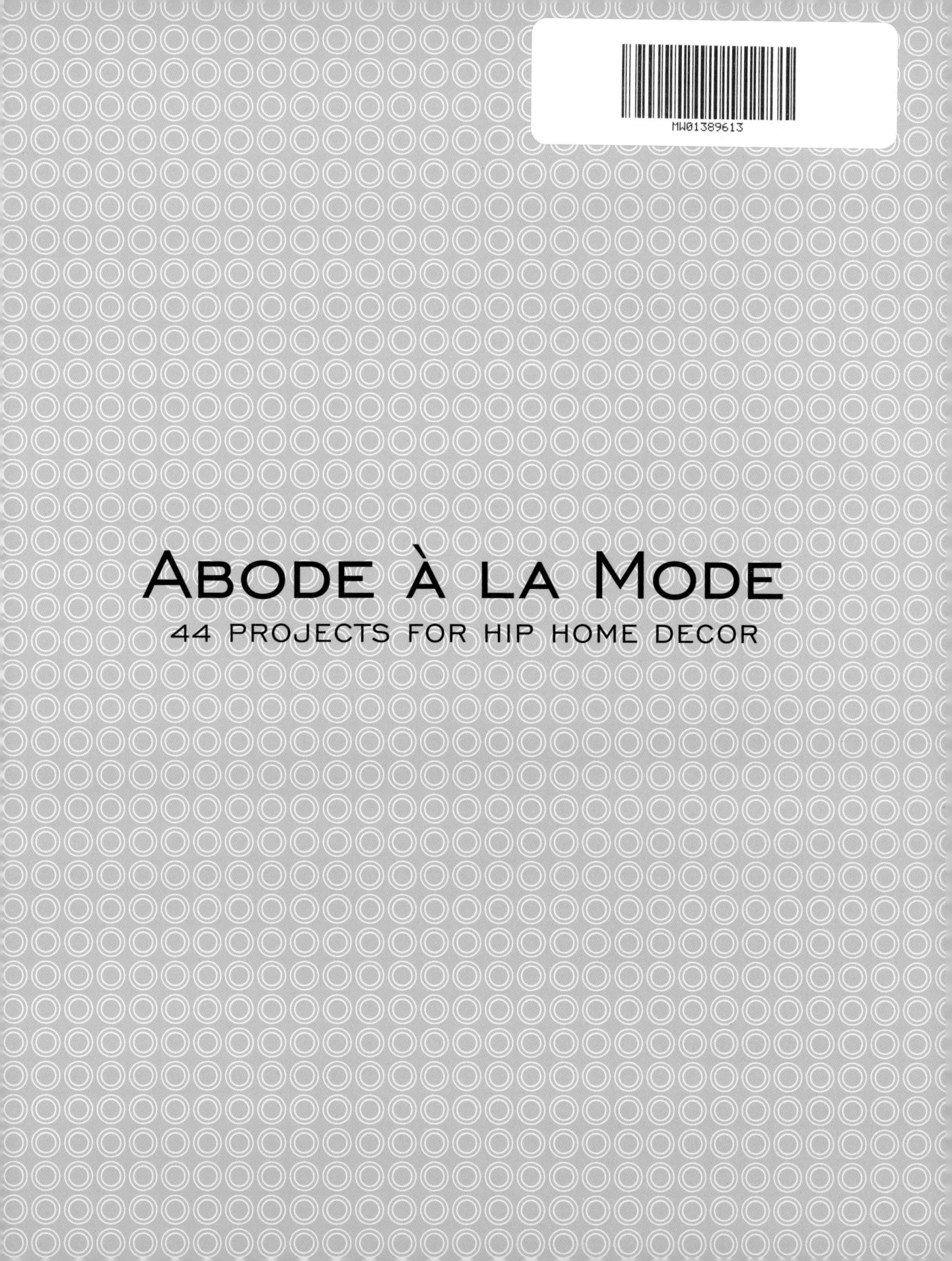

Abode à la Mode

44 Projects for Hip Home Decor

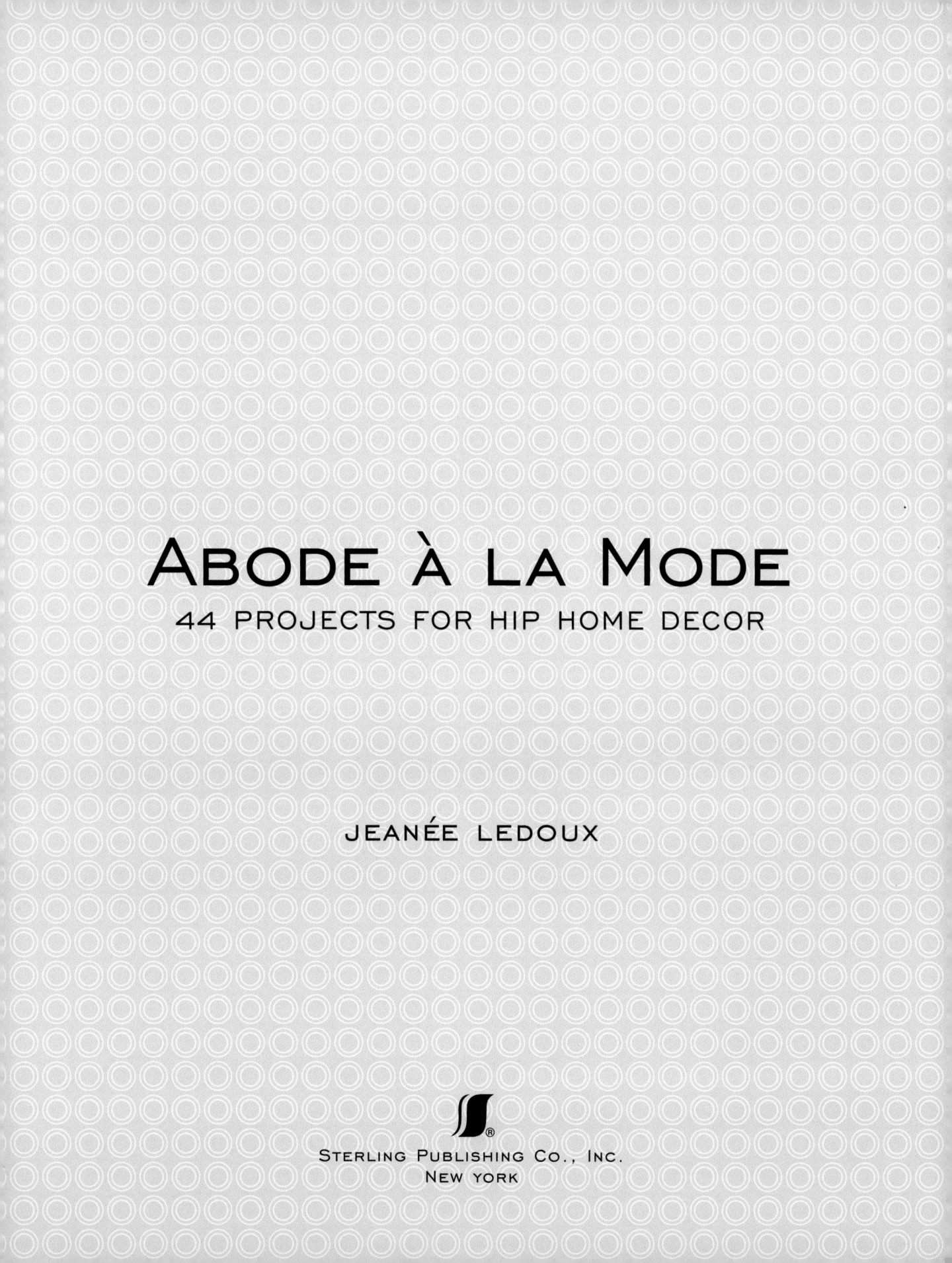

ABODE À LA MODE
44 PROJECTS FOR HIP HOME DECOR

JEANÉE LEDOUX

Sterling Publishing Co., Inc.
New York

Thanks to the following stores for providing props for this book: Mobilia, 43 Haywood Street, Asheville, NC, 28801, (828) 252-8322; Kosmos Designs, 49 N. Lexington Avenue, Asheville, NC 28801, (828) 281-0777; Terra Nostra Décor, 68 College Street, Asheville, NC 28801, (828) 252-9000.

Library of Congress Cataloging-in-Publication Data

Ledoux, Jeanée.
 Abode à la mode: 44 projects for hip home decor / Jeanée Ledoux.
   p. cm.
 Includes index.
 ISBN 1-4027-1343-6
 1. Handicraft. 2. House furnishings. 3. Interior decoration. I. Title.

TT157.L3285 2005
747—dc22

                                                    2005012392

10 9 8 7 6 5 4 3 2 1

Published by Sterling Publishing Co., Inc.
387 Park Avenue South, New York, NY 10016
© 2005 by Jeanée Ledoux
Distributed in Canada by Sterling Publishing
c/o Canadian Manda Group, 165 Dufferin Street
Toronto, Ontario, Canada M6K 3H6
Distributed in Great Britain by Chrysalis Books Group PLC
The Chrysalis Building, Bramley Road, London W10 6SP, England
Distributed in Australia by Capricorn Link (Australia) Pty. Ltd.
P.O. Box 704, Windsor, NSW 2756, Australia

Printed in China
All rights reserved

Sterling ISBN 1-4027-1343-6

For information about custom editions, special sales, premium and corporate purchases, please contact Sterling Special Sales Department at 800-805-5489 or specialsales@sterlingpub.com.

Family members, friends, and even strangers offered feedback, support, and tolerance that made this book possible. My parents believed in all my big ideas over the years and never doubted this one. Andrea empowered me from beginning to end, took a week off work to help with the photo shoot, and gave endless advice about hardware. My former roommates P. J., Casey, and Alicia let me take over our apartments with craft debris. P. J. designed my book proposal, and Charley volunteered to beat up the editors who rejected it. My Sterling editors gave a first-time author the chance she was waiting for and unexpected freedom. The staff of Lark Books and three Asheville homeowners lent their space and belongings for the photo shoot.

CONTENTS

INTRODUCTION 9

CHAPTER 1
DECORATING LOWDOWN 13

CHAPTER 2
WINDOWS 35
Polka-Dot Appliqué Panels 37
Studded Plum Sheer 39
Clip-Art Café Curtain 43
Upholstered Cardboard Valance 45
Fabric-Covered Roller Shade 49
Mondrian "Stained-Glass" Window 51
Lightbulb Curtain Finials 53

CHAPTER 3
LIGHTING 57
Plastic Mosaic Lamp Shade 59
Art Paper Tube Shade 61
Stacked Shade Lantern 65
Toilet-Inspired Torchère 69
Amoeba Box Light 71
Adjustable Globe Ceiling Fixture 74
Blueprint Sconce 79

CHAPTER 4
FURNITURE 83
Decoupaged Dresser 85
Woven Vinyl Headboard 89
Pizza Pan Pedestal 91

Low Sling Chair 95
Rolling Two-Tier Coffee Table 97
Slipcovered Crate Ottoman 101
Canvas Folding Screen 104
"Zebrawood" Bedside Tables 107
Recycled Drink Markers 111

· · · · ·

CHAPTER 5
WALLS AND FLOORS 113
Card Stock Wall Grid 115
Domino Backsplash 117
Fabric-Striped Wall 121
Memo Pad Mosaic Border 123
Painted Floorcloth 127
Faux Leopard Rug 130
Inlaid Faux Fur Rug 131

· · · · ·

CHAPTER 6
ACCESSORIES 135
Household Icons 137
Sunny Atomic Clock 139
Spray-Painted Bud Vases 143
Plastic Mesh Coasters 144
Mostly No-Sew Pillows 147
"Metal"-Framed Mirror with Vase 151
Retro Fridge Magnets 153

· · · · ·

CHAPTER 7
ART 155
3-D Pop Rocket 157
Trace-and-Cut Collage 159
Movable Magnetic Art 163
Celebrity Triptych 165
Soup Label Assembly 168
Masked Stripes Paintings 171
Gift Box Art 173
Index 174

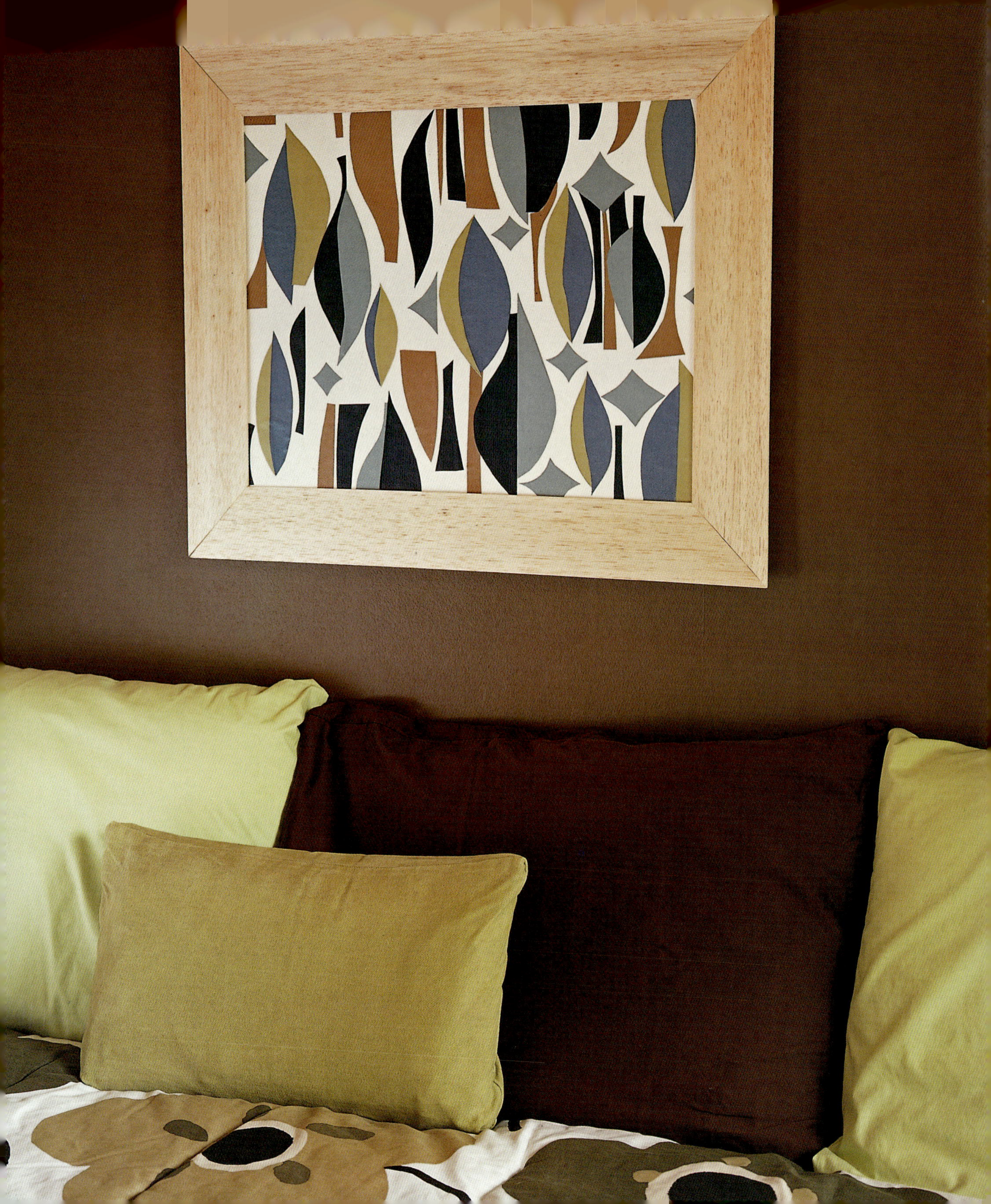

INTRODUCTION

This book is in your hands probably because an unadorned dwelling leaves you cold. You have too much attitude for bedrooms with plain white walls and living rooms furnished with plastic lawn chairs. You guffaw at ghostly fluorescent lighting and outdoor-grade carpeting. You're in firm disagreement with your roommates that beanbags, duct-taped posters, and string lights constitute Italian minimalism. "But we'll be here only a year or two," they whine when you measure for window treatments and take up a collection for an area rug. Time limits mean nothing to you, however, because you demand comfort and modern style even in the most temporary home. And why shouldn't you? You'll be relaxing, working, entertaining guests, and doing other essential activities in your personal space.

You have the drive to transform your little abode into a designer den, but the obstacles are many. Your free time and money are already stretched thin. Perhaps you're not allowed to paint the walls, replace the outdated flooring, or make other permanent changes. And then, as if these limitations weren't already shriveling your ambitions, you don't have the power tools—like a saw, drill, and sewing machine—necessary for so many inspiring projects in magazines and on TV. But before you lose your motivation and collapse onto your tattered sofa, read on. My book is all about finding solutions to surmount your decorating dilemmas.

I'm offering you the benefits of years of trial-and-error research carried out in my own dorm rooms and apartments. As an overworked and underdecorated college student, I dog-eared interiors magazines and mail-order catalogs and fantasized about a distant time when my space would reflect my passion for clean lines and retro Americana. I realized before long that I didn't have to wait; I didn't need to own a home or collect a six-figure salary. I could cheat my way to the look with a little cleverness, craftiness, and sweat. I gathered top-of-the-line materials like salvaged cardboard and plastic crates. I learned that the most basic, inexpensive (even free) supplies can be transformed into decorating gems with paint, fabric, art paper, and glue. Best of all, I developed projects that don't require out-of-our-league tools, only screwdrivers, glue guns, and other hand tools.

What's more, all my projects are reversible—no painted walls or wallpaper, no flooring fiascoes. Want color on the walls? How about fabric stripes that adhere with nothing more than spray starch? Need to cover unsightly stains on the floor? Whip up a high-end-look floorcloth that began life as a cheap cotton tablecloth. When it's moving time or you're hungry for a new look, your decorating escapades will leave no trace. You'll be maintenance-fee-free and armed to turn your next place into a house of style.

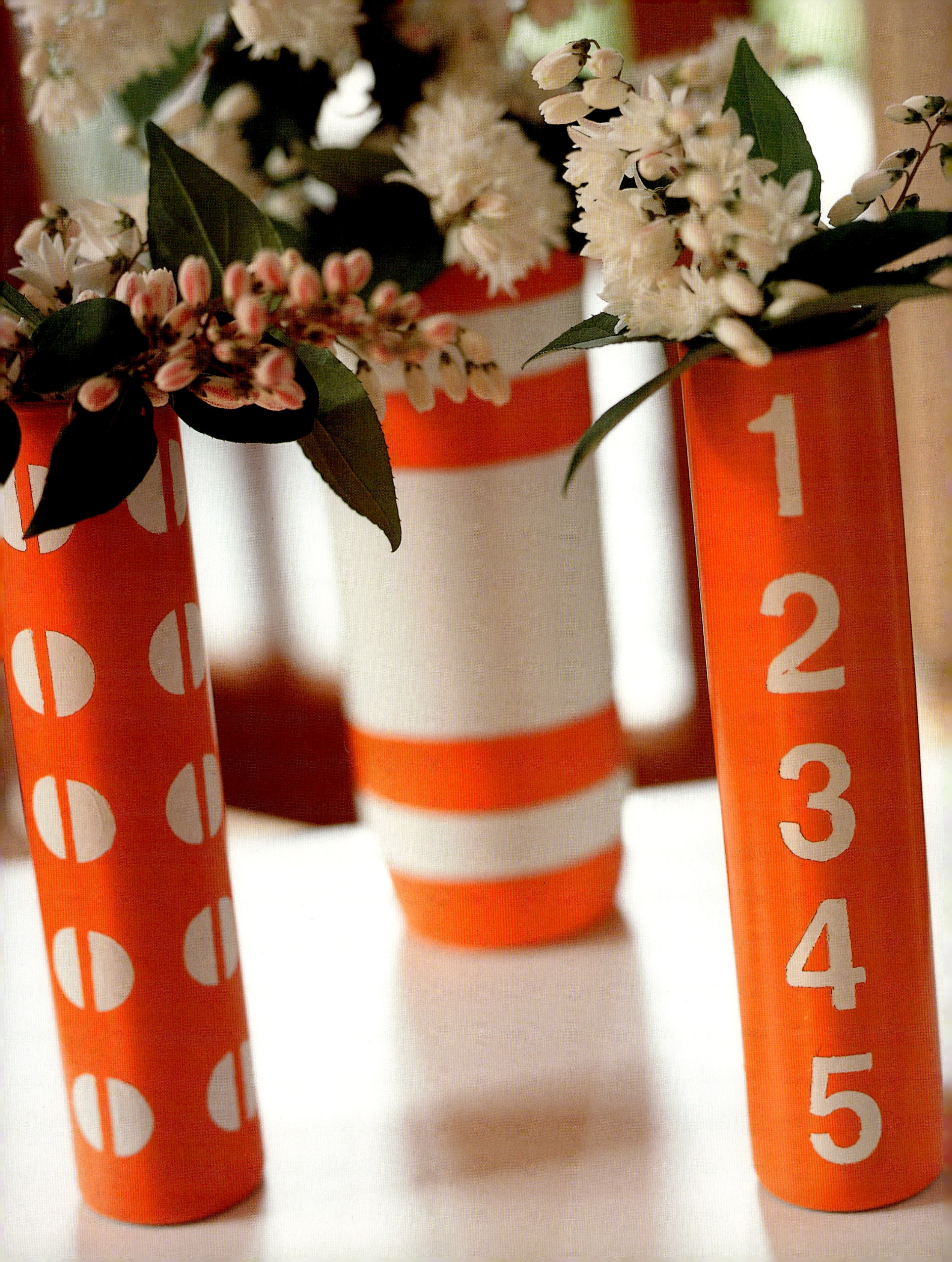
1
2
3
4
5

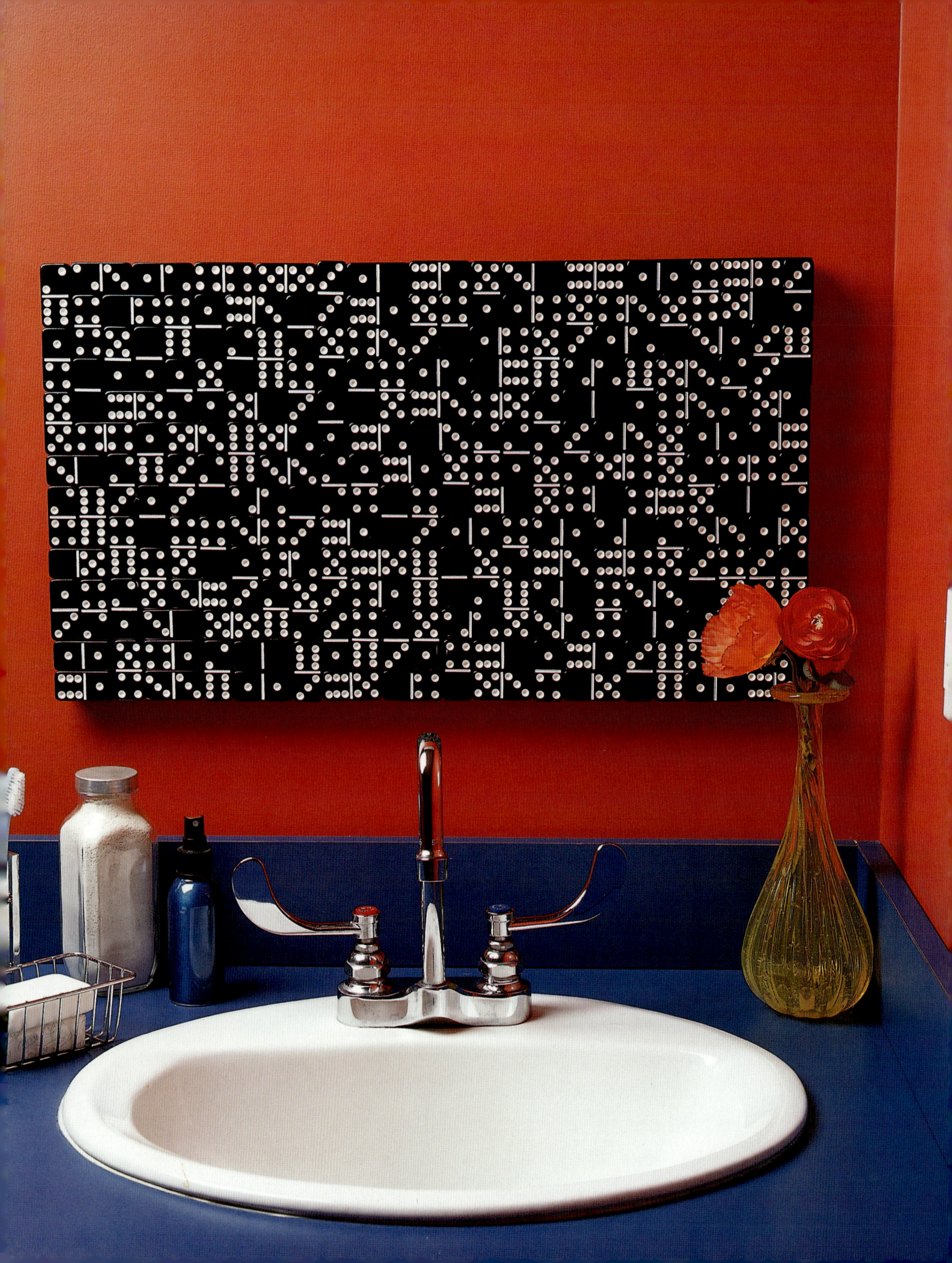

DECORATING LOWDOWN

Selecting an abode is all about compromise—the kitchen is tiny, but the local restaurants are great. The two fireplaces don't work, but the ceilings soar twelve feet high. Likewise, decorating is all about working within your space's and budget's (and perhaps your landlord's) limits. Knocking down walls and replacing the flooring may not be fair game, but you can carefully choose layouts, colors, furnishings, accessories, and more that make your dwelling a beautiful expression of your taste. Use the following guidelines to figure out what you like (possibly the hardest step), learn what each room can accommodate, work with the stuff you have, and inexpensively assemble a space that conveys a unique theme.

Get a Plan

If you want a great room, even if you're working with things you already own or you're crafting all the accoutrements, you need a great plan. That doesn't necessarily mean putting pencil to graph paper, but a finished-looking room will result only from a mind with a cohesive vision. If you don't have a master plan while you're buying, making, and arranging decor items, the outcome will feel flat and thrown together, no matter how impressive the individual pieces. And, of course, you'll spend extra money in the end to correct your mistakes. Flip through interiors books and magazines and you'll see that, despite the infinite diversity of decorating styles, the rooms created by professional beautifiers have a major quality in common: they look purposeful. All the elements harmonize and hang together, from the color of the fruit in the bowl to the arrangement of the books on the shelves. The creators chose certain pieces not because they were on sale or they've had them since high school, but simply because they worked. Like the beloved painter Bob Ross, you should be open to the occasional "happy accident" in your abode, but know that the real art of decorating is in exercising control.

The first step toward a decorating destination is to settle on a theme that suits your room's function. Let's get something straight: a themed room is not like a themed party. I'm not discussing explicit motifs such as "shrine to Elvis" or "1950s bowling alley," which are simple to achieve thanks to their over-the-top nature. I'm talking about something trickier, the subtle feeling your finished room will evoke. What do you want guests to utter when they enter? "Wow, your living room feels like a New York gallery," they might say, or an "after-hours lounge," a "cottage in the woods," an "intimate hotel." Let's take the example of the gallery motif. If that's what you want, visit some. Write down your likes and take pictures if you can. What are the common elements that would make your room feel gallerylike? Your interpretation doesn't have to be literal—a room filled with art but with no place to sit isn't functional or fun. What about one fantastic piece of art as a focal point, with upholstered benches in front where visitors can relax and ponder the painting or sculpture as well as gaze at a television or fireplace? What else inspires you about galleries? Openness, clean lines, muted background colors? All these things can be translated into your room.

Once you've done your on-site research and are bursting with ideas, don't go tearin' up the showrooms yet. Tear up magazines and books instead. Cut out photos and dog-ear pages, then live with the pictures for a while. Resource materials are much less expensive than impulsively purchased furnishings, so gaze at them until blindness sets in or you can't stomach seeing another sofa. Draw arrows and write notes in the margins about what appeals, where it would go, the alternative color you want it in, and so on. And don't ignore the advertisements: companies that buy space in interiors periodicals spend oodles on their picturesque campaigns, hiring the best art directors, stylists, and photographers in the business, and you can benefit from their talents for free.

A clean, sparse seating area inspired by a painting.

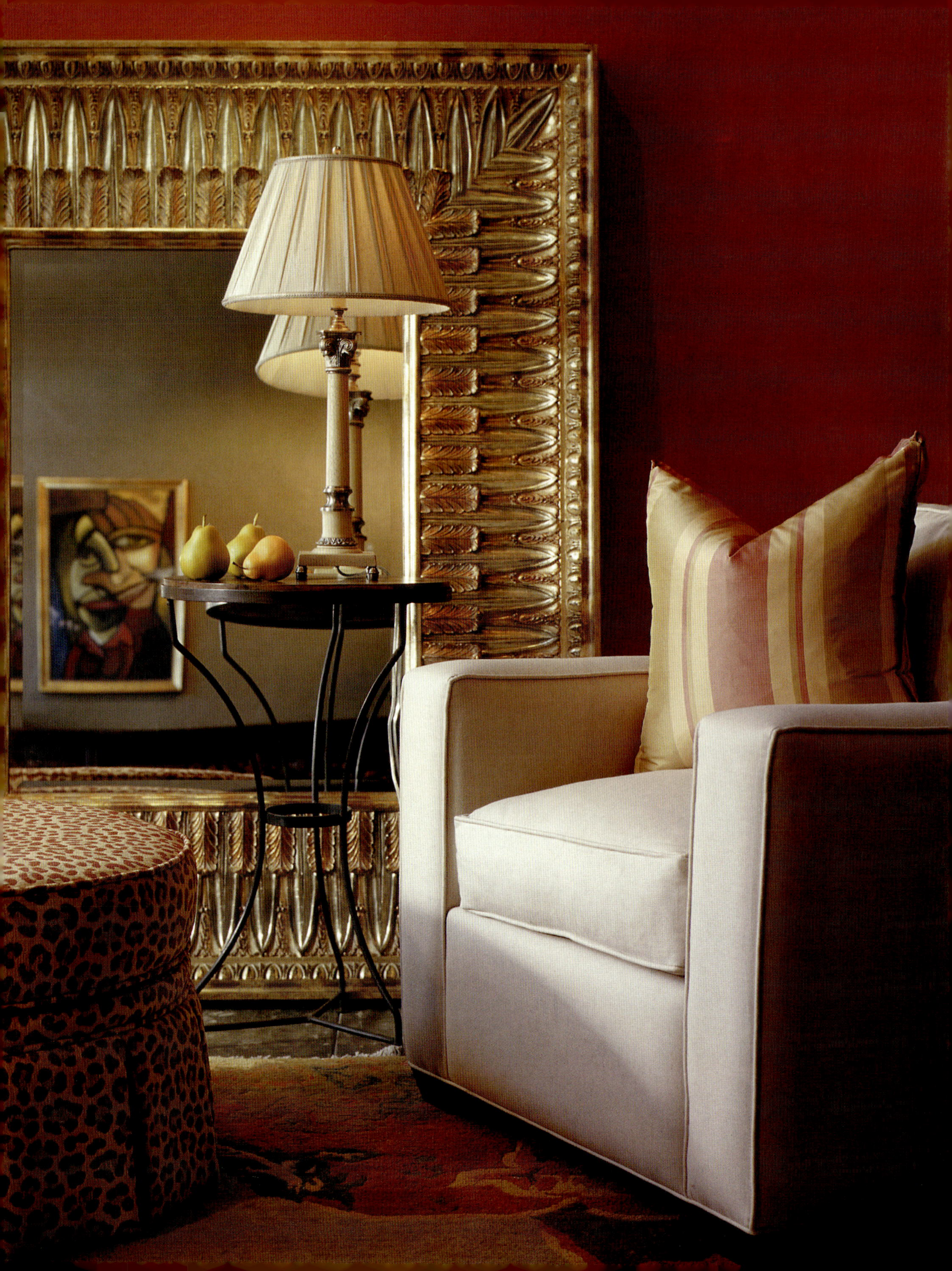

Since your theme is general and can be visually expressed in countless ways, your current task is to zero in on how you will do that. A room filled with black furniture can evoke the same sorts of feelings as one decked out in white, and tall floor lamps can achieve the same aesthetic as low-hanging lanterns, so which style do you prefer? What patterns of taste are emerging from all those piles of paper you've accumulated? Are you noticing that you always fell for boxy instead of elliptical tables, that you selected solid colors over busy fabric patterns, that you preferred streamlined loungers to fluffy armchairs? Run your findings by anyone who will be sharing the decorated space with you, blend your tastes if you must, then move on to the next phase.

Once you know what you like, begin the transition from general to specific. Select one item to be your tangible inspiration. Pick out a beloved object from your personal stash or from a store to reflect the theme of the entire room. Beginning the decorating process with a single rug, painting, vase, or fabric swatch is a good way to keep yourself focused, much as writing an outline keeps an essay on target. The inspiration item should express the spirit of your room and display most or all of the colors you will use, which is why textiles and artwork serve better than, say, a piece of wooden furniture. They are artist's palettes that you can refer to when you're feeling confused or overwhelmed. Will this chartreuse chair fit in with my theme? But of course, it looks smashing with my inspiration piece. The pivotal item can be small and doesn't have to occupy a prominent place in the room. Think of it as a template, not necessarily a centerpiece. Have it or its picture with you when you're researching.

If you have a paint chip in your hand, drop it immediately and reread the previous paragraph. A rectangular swatch of paint *cannot* be your inspiration. Starting your room with a wall color and then trying to find everything else to match—furniture, pillows, curtains, artwork—is backward. This oft-practiced folly leads only to frustration and possibly repainting. Since you can have paint mixed in any shade, it just makes sense to begin with a unique object that's the springboard for your room's colors. We'll talk more about wall color a little later.

This room's furniture and accessories were selected based on the palette and spirit of the inspiration piece: the painting.

Scope Your Room

You're getting closer to hearing the cash register ring, but do a little more planning first. You have to evaluate your room's structure before you can decide how you will fill it. Empty it out if you can, measure the walls, then subtract from those dimensions any space that you need to leave around a hearth, a door that opens into the space, a bookshelf, and so on. (Eighteen inches is usually enough to allow a body to pass.) Such features that are part of the bones of your room chip away at the actual area available to furnish. Also note any space bonuses, such as a niche or bay window. You don't have to draw a floor plan, but be aware of your room's "real" dimensions when you're brainstorming and shopping. Is the space that you're left with large enough to create multiple conversation areas? Deep enough to put furniture into the center of the room rather than against walls? Where are the windows and lighting fixtures?

Next take a long look at your vacant room and try to get a sense of its inherent personality. Though naked, it still has character, just like your naked body has birthmarks and distinctive curves. Does the shape feel intimate or airy? Does the room have details such as fancy molding, a rustic fireplace, a formal chandelier, or whimsical doorknobs that are injecting a certain feel? If the feeling evoked does not mesh with your theme, can you make adjustments to these elements?

Now that you have a better idea of what you want and what your room can accommodate, it's time to look at what you already own. Your checking account isn't bottomless, and you probably have at least a few things with sentimental or monetary value. Do they already work with your theme? If not, can they be tweaked or transformed to fit in? Sometimes the smallest adjustment can revolutionize the look of a piece, such as changing a sideboard's drawer pulls or giving a sofa new accent pillows. On the more drastic end of things, a shabby-chic coffee table with straight lines could be made to look modern with a paint treatment that mimics brushed steel, and an armchair could undergo a double amputation to be reborn as a slipper chair. Gather up your inspirational pictures and compare them to your stuff to see what has the potential to evolve.

> ### WHEN YOU'RE STUCK WITH UGLY STUFF
>
> Part of your abode's decorating destiny, unfortunately, may be predetermined by a previous occupant's bad taste or your landlord's neglect. For example, your kitchen has avocado linoleum from 1972, or your bathroom hosts a pukey pink commode and tub. If you can't renovate or cover them up, your instincts will tell you to work against these displeasing fixtures, to decorate as if they don't exist. But if you don't integrate them into your design, you're only exaggerating their presence and creating disharmony. Suck it up and make the tacky standout your inspiration piece. Base your color scheme, accessories, and so on around the offensive item so that your whole room looks pulled together and purposeful. In other words, make lemonade.

Create Harmony

Try this exercise before you commit to your room's major players. Put pictures of the furnishings you're considering together on a white background, then squint. When the shapes blur, you're left gazing at a series of surfaces. You'll probably see some combo of fabric, stained wood, metal, glass, plastic, paint, and stone. Think of every different surface as an element. (A black metal is not the same element as a silver metal, and the same goes for a patterned fabric versus a solid fabric, a dark-stained wood versus a light-stained wood, and so on.) How many different elements do you count? Too many makes for chaos, and what you want is control, so edit down to a smaller number of coordinating finishes if necessary. The ones that make the cut must relate to each other like brothers and sisters. To avoid sibling rivalry, your pieces need characteristics in common. If you want to arrange, say, a sofa, a coffee table, and two chairs plus accessories in a sitting area, the pieces don't have to be from the same set or even be classified as the same style, but they do have to harmonize. For example, the key pieces in my living room (see page 27) have no shared heritage—I purchased the sofa new, built the coffee table from shelving boards and plumbing parts, and recovered the vintage chairs—but they live together happily because they're united by mutual traits.

This fabric trio harmonizes thanks to the common colors and the non-competing scales and rhythms of pattern.

Think not only about your pieces' similarities but also their complementary differences. Achieving harmony means balancing opposites as well as grouping likes. Offset boxy shapes with curves, textured surfaces with smooth ones, and so on. An oval mirror, womblike vases, and a circular pedestal table can bring the right balance to a room that's dominated by straight-lined furnishings. Likewise, a fuzzy shag rug can modishly play yin to the yang of a smooth acrylic coffee table.

Fabrics can be the wiliest elements to coordinate. They're probably an essential expression of your room's theme, but they won't sing harmonious duets unless you put together patterns correctly. Designers of traditional interiors offer this guideline: combine one floral, one stripe, and one solid. This narrow advice can be expanded to any type and number of fabric patterns when you understand the reasoning behind it. Florals and stripes make good companions because they don't compete, and a solid field of color never offended any of its neighboring textiles. Flowers, leaves, vines, and the like are curvy and have an organic rhythm, meaning that your eye dances all over the pattern when you see it. Stripes, by contrast, have a rigid shape and lead your eye in only one direction. Finally, a solid color serves as a distraction-free surface on which your peepers can rest. In other words, the fabrics in a grouping must have distinctly different effects on you, the viewer, for harmony to reign. The patterns you mix should have diverse scales and rhythms, such as a pillow covered in two-inch squares paired with a throw adorned with four-inch-wide wavy lines. The same small squares could also sit pretty next to very large squares. Your "solid" fabric (perhaps the sofa behind the pillow and throw) may have a subtle tone-on-tone pattern, or any sort of texture you like.

Tweak Your Colors

If you're building your room around a carefully selected inspiration item, you already know what colors you want to work with. Let's say you're pulling your hues from a platter painted olive green, brick red, and dusty yellow. All you have to do is decide what scale you want to see each color in. For large and expensive furniture items, most people feel comfortable with neutral and/or subtle colors such as olive, tan, gray, and white and reserve stronger colors such as red and yellow for accessories and artwork. Swapping out accent pieces is the easiest way to refresh a room's look, so restricting bold colors to lightweight, inexpensive items is a good idea if you crave change often.

If you will be painting, the room's inspiration item determines the range of possibilities for your wall color as well. You can go lighter or darker or slightly side to side on the color spectrum, if you like. To choose the right hue, consider a couple of things. First, does the room have a problem of size or natural light that you want to address? Is it an open, sun-drenched space that you want to feel smaller and more cozy? Demonstrating with the palette above, choose from the red or olive family to make the walls less reflective and feel nearer. Is the room small and cavelike? Go with yellow paint to bounce light around the area and make the walls visually recede. Second, do you want the background color to have its own show or to play a subtle supporting role for the surrounding furnishings? An olive couch and a red wall are complementary, each making the other more intense. The same couch

Modern furnishings such as this boxy chair can be harmoniously grouped with other styles if the pieces are united by color.

backed by a lighter greenish-khaki wall, however, draws all attention to itself.

Your color palette can help to make your home seamless on a small and large scale. Furniture styles that conflict can be happily married if they have color in common. For example, I saw a photo of a boxy, rustic, hand-painted chest, probably an antique from Central America, sitting next to a sleek and slippery leather chair. They weren't misfits, though, thanks to yellow. The bright canary of the chair meshed harmoniously with the chipping yellow and other primary pigments on the chest. Color is also the key to making one room flow into the next. Painting each room the same hue but varying the accent colors is an elementary but surefire strategy. You can also make one area's main color an accent color in the next, then that room's main color an accent in the next, and so on. If each room will be a different color, you can ensure harmony by selecting them all from a manufacturer's collection, a family of colors assembled under a theme such as "southwestern desert" (warm, earthy colors) or "beachfront" (cool, watery colors).

MAKING WHITE WALLS WORK

Rooms with standard white walls often look unfinished, as if someone was just about to put on a colorful coat of paint when you walked in. If your landlord won't let you paint, don't sweat it. A white backdrop can be lovely if your decorating works with it instead of against it. Try one of these solutions:

- Rather than decorating in spite of it—using every color except white in a room—prominently incorporate white into your accent pieces to make the walls and ceiling look purposeful. Use white in artwork, vases, lamp shades, candles, and so on.

- Some of the most striking interiors use white exclusively. Monochromatic schemes work best when you layer many shades and textures, such as a buttery shag rug under a snow-white vinyl sofa draped with a beige-and-ivory-striped wool throw.

- Use a white wall as a backdrop for a colorful treatment you apply on top, such as the card stock grid on page 115 and the fabric stripes on page 121.

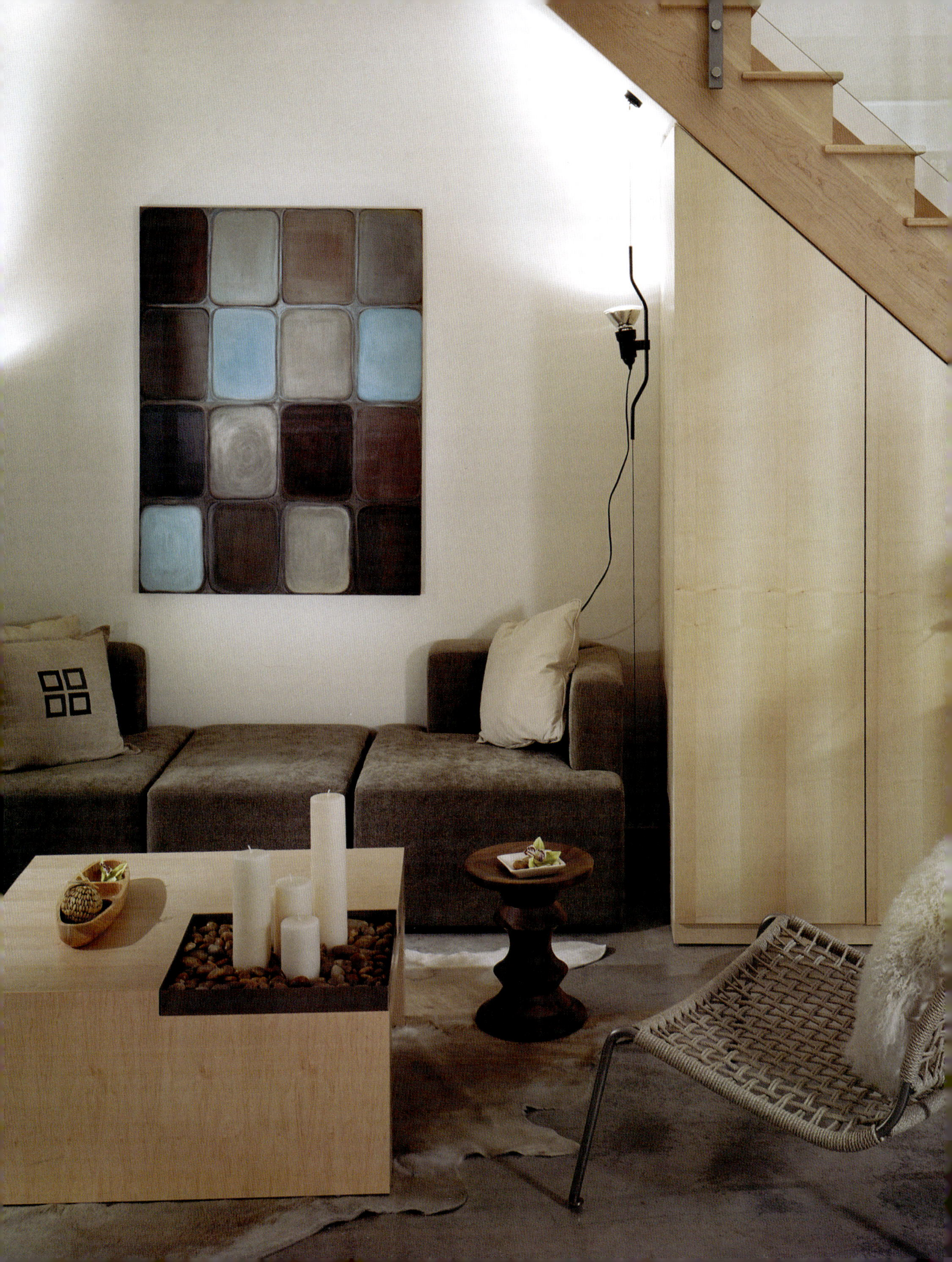

Judge color contenders in your space, not at a store, whenever possible. Under a hardware or fabric dealer's flickering artificial light, you can't tell how yellowy a green is or how orangy a red. You'll see the true hues in your room's light next to your room's stuff. And don't choose your paint color from a minuscule chip alone; buy a quart and paint a patch. Taking a shortcut won't save you money—I'm the queen of sheepishly returned gallons because I jumped the gun. For fabrics, cut free swatches if you can or purchase a quarter of a yard. For furniture and rugs, order samples from manufacturers.

Choose Your Furniture

It's only a well-tailored bundle of fabric, foam, and springs, but furniture is the most important element for expressing your room's theme. It's also the most expensive. If you're skipping ahead and haven't done your homework, go back to "Scope Your Room" to figure out your room's needs before you buy. A great sofa loses its charm in a room that's too small to hold it, mind you, so slow down and get a firm plan. Furniture purchases require more consideration than any other decorating decision, but your patience will be rewarded with the right pieces that, if high quality, can stick with you for a decade or more.

Balance Quality and Economy

Furniture can really bite into your budget, but knowing where to splurge and where to skimp helps. I suggest going all out for a room's most important piece, such as the sofa in a living room, and opting for handmade or salvaged supplementary furnishings. Accent tables and lightweight chairs are for experimentation, for testing your craftiness and thriftiness, but not so larger items like sofas. Don't drag in that rained-on, beat-up couch from the street and expect to transform it. I've seen it a hundred times: you'll throw a too-small tapestry over it in defeat after you realize that you're no upholsterer and shouldn't have bought all that expensive fabric that now lies in pieces in the bottom of your closet. Save your money and go for the real thing; you'll never regret it.

TRANSFORM AN OFFICE CHAIR

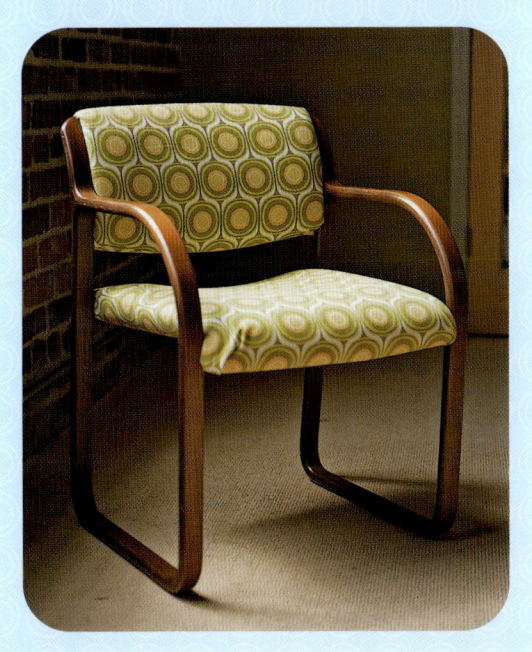

You've probably sat on chairs like this one countless times—in a doctor's office, a dorm room, an airport. You may see such seats bargain-priced at office surplus stores or yard sales, but their dusty upholstery gives no cause for a second glance. Try to look beyond the blah to what the chair does have going for it: the simple lines are nice, and it's easy to take apart and re-cover with any fabric you like. Poke your head under the seat and check out the screws. If their heads are in good shape (not stripped), you're in business.

Remove the seat's screws and pop it off. The chair's back probably doesn't have visible hardware, but rather a thin covering made of plastic or metal that hides it. Use a flathead screwdriver to pry off the covering, which is most likely held on with rubber nuts that may break. That's all right. Remove the now-exposed screws and pop off the back cushion.

The two cushions are likely backed with wood, so you can staple new fabric right over the old. Cut out a piece that's several inches larger than the cushion all around so you can wrap it underneath. Start with a staple in the middle of one edge, then pull the fabric taut and put a staple in the opposite edge. Move an inch from your first staple and apply another, then another on the opposite edge. Continue in this way to keep the fabric from puckering, but leave the corners for last. Make hospital folds, as with bedsheets, to hide the excess fabric at the corners and staple them. When you have re-covered both cushions, reattach them to the chair frame.

For the back covering, use pliers to remove any remaining rubber nuts. Stretch the fabric over it, using hot glue instead of staples. Glue or nail the covering to the back cushion.

Still haven't snapped out of your scavenging ways? Here's a dark tale of dissuasion: A few years ago I bought a contemporary sofa at a deep discount because it had a tear in its back, a burn hole in one arm, and—gasp—it was missing its middle seat cushion. The first two problems weren't terrible, but one-third of the sofa's tush support was absent, a fatal flaw that should have driven me away. Still unable to resist thrift, I decided to purchase the sofa and make a replacement cushion. I found a close fabric match, but, predictably, the prosthetic seat never pulled its weight. Its foam wasn't dense enough and quickly became saggy, and the substitute chenille faded to a dusty pink while its surroundings remained cherry. On top of that, the tear and burn hole grew as people's weight put stress on the fabric. I didn't save any money with my discount couch, because after a year I was ready to sell my pathetic patient for the cost of a nice meal.

Many people rescue distressed sofas with the intention of slipcovering them. While this technique does hide the most hideous upholstery, it's still not a good long-term solution. First, mass-produced slipcovers usually hang like muumuus because they're made to fit a huge variety of shapes and sizes. No matter how vigilantly you tuck and straighten, they work themselves into baggy sacks. Second, while custom-made slipcovers fit better, they're expensive. The average sofa requires sixteen to twenty yards of fabric, so you do the math. Why not put that money toward a perfect piece that needs no tweaking or covering?

Reserve thriftiness for surrounding furniture pieces, such as office-type chairs with removable seats and backs that you can staple new fabric onto (see page 25 for directions). Build items from scratch with humble ingredients such as electrical conduit, plastic crates, and plumbing parts. Coffee tables, upholstered cubes, and other supplementary furnishings can rotate in and out of your decor to keep things fresh and provide you with a chance to experiment.

Here's why this room works:

- The room's inspiration piece, the pair of paintings, provided the color palette and clean, contemporary feeling.
- The sofa, chairs, coffee table, and accent table are different styles, but they're united by their chrome-colored metal legs.
- Gray, brown, blue, and white move around the room in various shades.
- The three fabric patterns in the room share colors but have different scales and rhythms and therefore harmonize.
- The white table, lamps, and square pillows help the white walls and ceiling to look purposeful.
- The furniture floats away from the walls, creating a sense of airiness, and the V-shaped arrangement is conducive to conversation.
- Every seated guest has a nearby surface on which to set things.
- The shaggy leather rug, fuzzy alpaca throw, and rough ceramic flowerpot add texture to a room dominated by smooth surfaces.
- The curvy accent table, chair legs, glass vase, and ceramic flowerpot balance the room's straight lines.
- The two lamps in opposite corners and the recessed bulbs in the ceiling ensure that the room is bathed in light.
- The tree, fern, and flowers contribute the warmth of living things.

Make the Arrangement

The arrangement you choose for your furnishings may be as important as the items themselves. There's little point in owning an oh-so-fabulous sofa if your guests stumble into its back when they enter your abode. A room with well-placed pieces feels natural, as if it couldn't be laid out any other way, and guests won't stumble unless you're too generous with the cocktails. Position your furniture to help traffic flow, induce conversation, and define a room's different functions.

A room should feel open and welcoming from all its entrances. People shouldn't have to look directly at pieces' backs, and they should have access to multiple seats without walking a U- or L-shaped path. Bring a sense of airiness to even the smallest room by allowing enough space around all furnishings for a body to pass (at least eighteen inches), and avoid putting any items in contact with the wall. If one or more seats must go against a wall because of space constraints, leave a few inches for a floating appearance. Backless and armless furniture (benches, chaises, ottomans, and slipper chairs) is a boon in cramped quarters because it helps guests to weave about fluidly and orient themselves in different directions.

Once they find their seats, your visitors want to chat, set down their glasses, and put their feet up. Find a balance between maintaining adequate passageways between furniture and bringing sitters close enough to see and hear each other easily. Also position surfaces such as tables and ottomans so that guests can reach them without stretching too far or standing up. If television watching is on the agenda, make sure no one has to turn her head too far. Incorporate some swiveling or wheeled pieces if the tube is not in everyone's view. A classic arrangement that fulfills these criteria is a sofa and two chairs that form a square with a long coffee table in the center (figure 1a). A more casual approach is to set the sofa and chairs catercorner around a central table for a cozy triangular shape (figure 1b). For a room primarily used for socializing, not TV watching, an X shape formed by four chairs and a central table makes an edgy grouping that allows equal access from every direction (figure 1c).

These days many dwellings have rooms that must perform double

Figure 1a
Traditional square arrangement

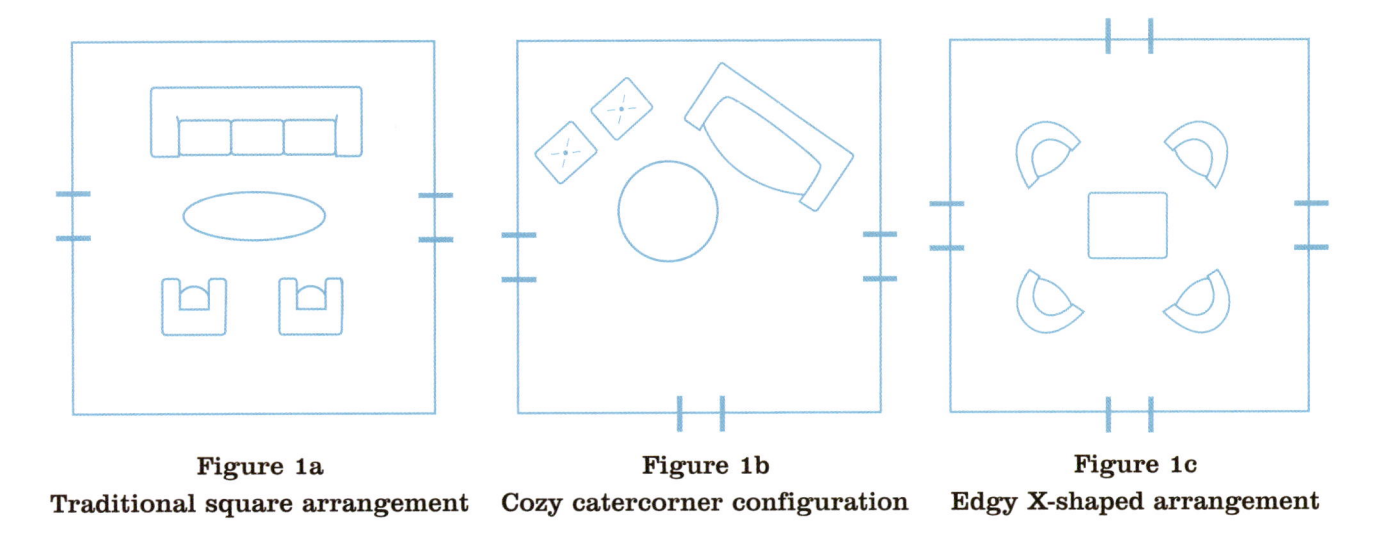

Figure 1b
Cozy catercorner configuration

Figure 1c
Edgy X-shaped arrangement

or triple duty—the living and dining rooms are combined, or a bedroom includes a home office. If you live in a studio, you have the special challenge of doing everything except powdering your nose in one box. Furniture arrangement is the answer to creating distinct areas in combination spaces. Use the lines of your seating and the boundaries of rugs to create rooms within rooms. For example, separate lounging grounds from eating quarters by using the back of a sofa as a low wall. I know, I just said that guests entering a room should not stare into the monster's back, but those seated at the dining table will appreciate the division and will have other pretty things to focus on, such as your chandelier and linens.

Garnish with Accessories

The accessories in your room serve the same functions as the ones on your body: they add color, direct eyes where you want them, and project your personality. If you have the means, splurge on a painting or other focal point you love, but balance a room with low-budget accessories as you would balance an outfit with costume jewelry. Both add lots of punch and can be cycled out when you want to change your look. Accessories offer a chance to be bold and daring without financial regrets. So, if you're a rouge lover, you might pass on red armchairs but snatch up red throw pillows without a thought, right? The latter are

Begin accessorizing a room by grouping like objects into a collection.

comparatively inexpensive and can be re-covered easily if you decide to take your room's accents from toasty to cool. Crazy about a fabric with a funky floral pattern? Don't use it to re-cover your sofa. Buy a remnant and wrap it around a lamp shade.

For me, laying out a room's accent pieces is the most exciting part of decorating, the home stretch, but it's also easy to goof at this stage. A wildly popular strategy is simply to pepper each available surface with every knickknack collected over the years. Fight the temptation to clutter by using the first rule of accessorizing: thoughtfully edit your possessions. Each tchotchke should work within your theme and relate to the surrounding furnishings in terms of scale and placement. A husky bureau needs some visually weighty accents, for example, not a sprinkling of delicate figurines. And hanging pictures should be oriented around furnishings placed against that wall, not arbitrarily centered at eye level.

Start with any collections you have and build around those groupings. If you're thinking, "Collections? Like dolls and model airplanes? That's for kids and old people," let me inform you that you probably already have multiple collections in your home, but the items are in different rooms and aren't connected in your mind. Nevertheless, they tell a story about you and your roommates, especially when they're displayed together. A collection can be a mere three objects that have something in common, such as material (clay vessels), era (1950s Americana), or theme (movie keepsakes). Case in point: my boyfriend the photographer has a hand-crank movie camera and an old leather case for a still camera. I like the look of these antiques and wanted to display them, but I needed a third item for balance. I dug through my college darkroom kit and discovered a metal film canister with cool lettering and a worn finish. Voilà—a photography collection. Wipe the dust bunnies off your unrealized collections and display them.

Aim for visual balance when you're arranging accessories. Making symmetrical layouts is the most elementary way to achieve this, but symmetry can feel formal and uninteresting. For instance, a bed flanked by identical side tables and reading lamps evens out Libra's scales and pleases the eye, but it's not always practical or desirable to own everything in twos. You can achieve a more complex and intriguing balance by corralling objects based on common as well as complementary traits, just as you did when selecting furniture. To illustrate, in the photo on page 32, the glass vases on the left and the glass-shaded lamps on the right share an ethereal, manufactured feeling, while the wooden bowl between them feels heavy and primitive by contrast. Experiment with what you own, including everyday objects that may not currently have accessory status—stacks of books, colorful shoes, your favorite album covers—to make asymmetrical harmony. Combine related objects, but also pair squatty with tall, clear with opaque, and so on. Play with varying amounts of empty space around the accents. You can also move background pieces such as wall art to the left or right to balance the foreground arrangement.

> Living things add a special warmth to decor, especially in a contemporary space. Use plants of various heights, colors, and textures as you do other accessories.

Illuminate Your Space

All that remains is to cast a flattering glow over the beautiful elements you've assembled. Chances are, you have a single overhead light that's killing your room softly, no matter how divine your furniture and accessories, for three reasons. First, it makes the space appear gloomy

Here's why these accessories work:

- The credenza's ends, though asymmetrical, are balanced by the objects' materials (glass and chrome) and vertical orientation.
- Placing the two lamps together instead of at either end provides a surprise and draws attention to their sculptural quality rather than their function.
- The primitive wooden bowl offers a pleasing contrast with the ethereal vases and lamps.
- The painting's position to the right of center balances the surface's visually weightier left side.
- The collection of Thai silk pouches in the bowl reflects the colors in the painting.
- The books add weight and height where needed and didn't cost a thing.

around the edges. The good stuff isn't only in the middle of the room, but that's what the solo bulb implies. Second, a blanket of light from above gives no direction to viewers below, so your guests' eyes will graze the room in a meandering way. Don't you want them to focus immediately on your new painting? Your ceramics collection? Third, people look more attractive when they're basking in light from a lower level. Turn on that hanging fixture when you're cleaning, not socializing.

Create pockets of light instead of an all-or-nothing setup. When varying amounts of light come from distinct areas, the effect is a path leading the eyes around the room. Light behaves like an intense color, beckoning, "Hey, look here! Now over here!" Artwork and collections are obvious choices for spotlights and recessed lights in shelving. A chair intended for reading should have a lamp nearby, and a work area might have a few low pendant lights. The very bones of your room might be worthy of illumination as well. Highlight the millwork around your fireplace, throw a shower up to your ceiling's exposed beams, or direct a gooseneck spotlight down a brick wall to make its pockmarks pop. If smooth plasterboard walls and ceilings are your fate, try vertically lighting a large plant or a favorite piece of furniture to cast interesting shadows.

How about making the light source itself a feast for the eyes? A fixture can be a striking object in which the bulb is merely a bonus. On the high end, turn a dark corner into a gallery with a hand-blown glass shade with swirled colors. On the low end, use a free blueprint mounted on plastic as a shade for a sconce (see page 79). Make a statement with a gobo, a fixture that projects words or pictures onto a wall for a mural-like effect. You can buy one with a prefab image or make one using a spotlight and aluminum foil with cutouts.

Living in a place you don't own doesn't mean being limited to lamps. Swap out boring built-in fixtures for stylish ones with equivalent voltage, then reswap when you move. For ultimate flexibility in directing light, try a cable system with clip-on lights that plugs into the wall instead of being wired to a ceiling box like a traditional track system. Some versions have stiff wire conductors that you can bend into sculptural shapes such as circles and waves.

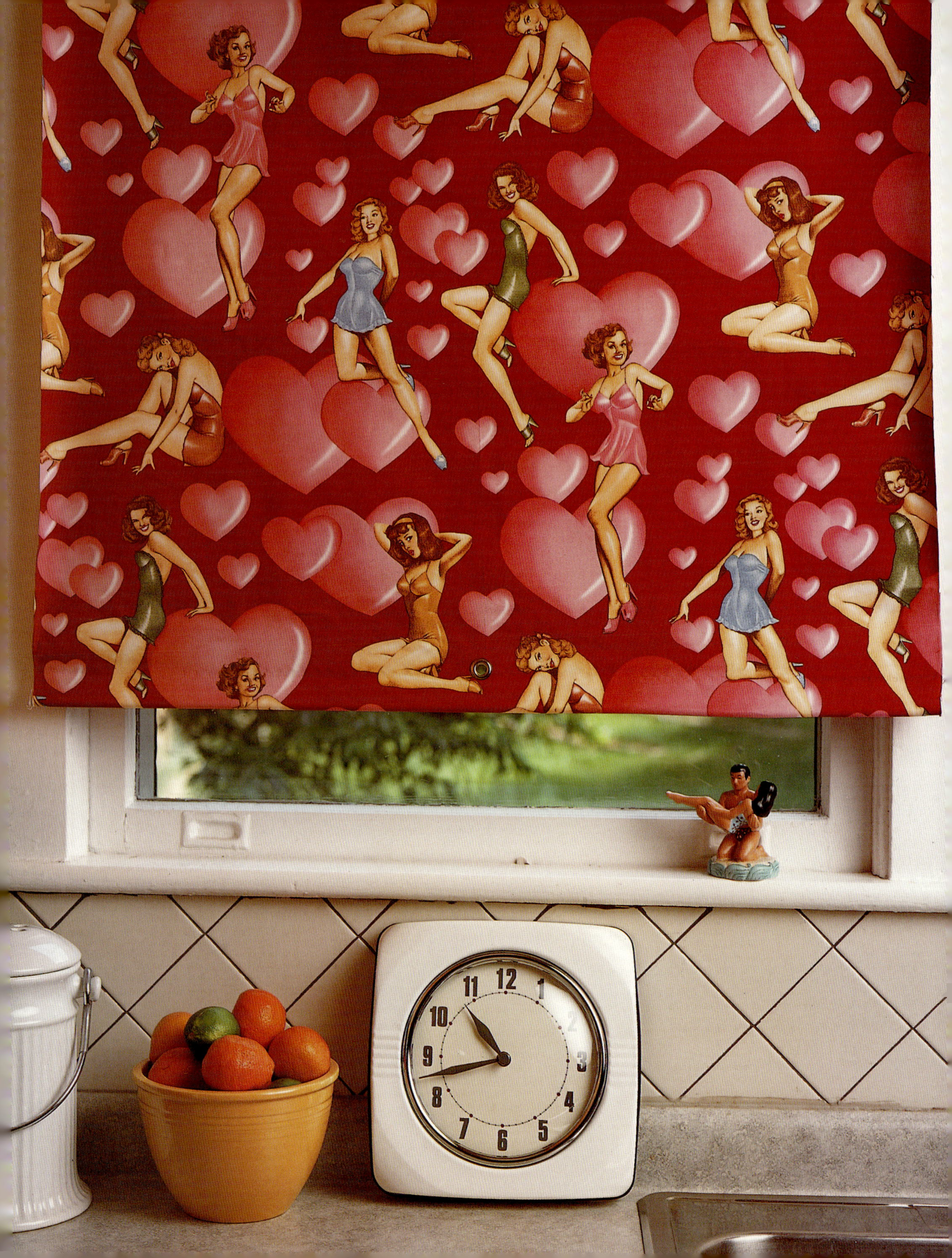

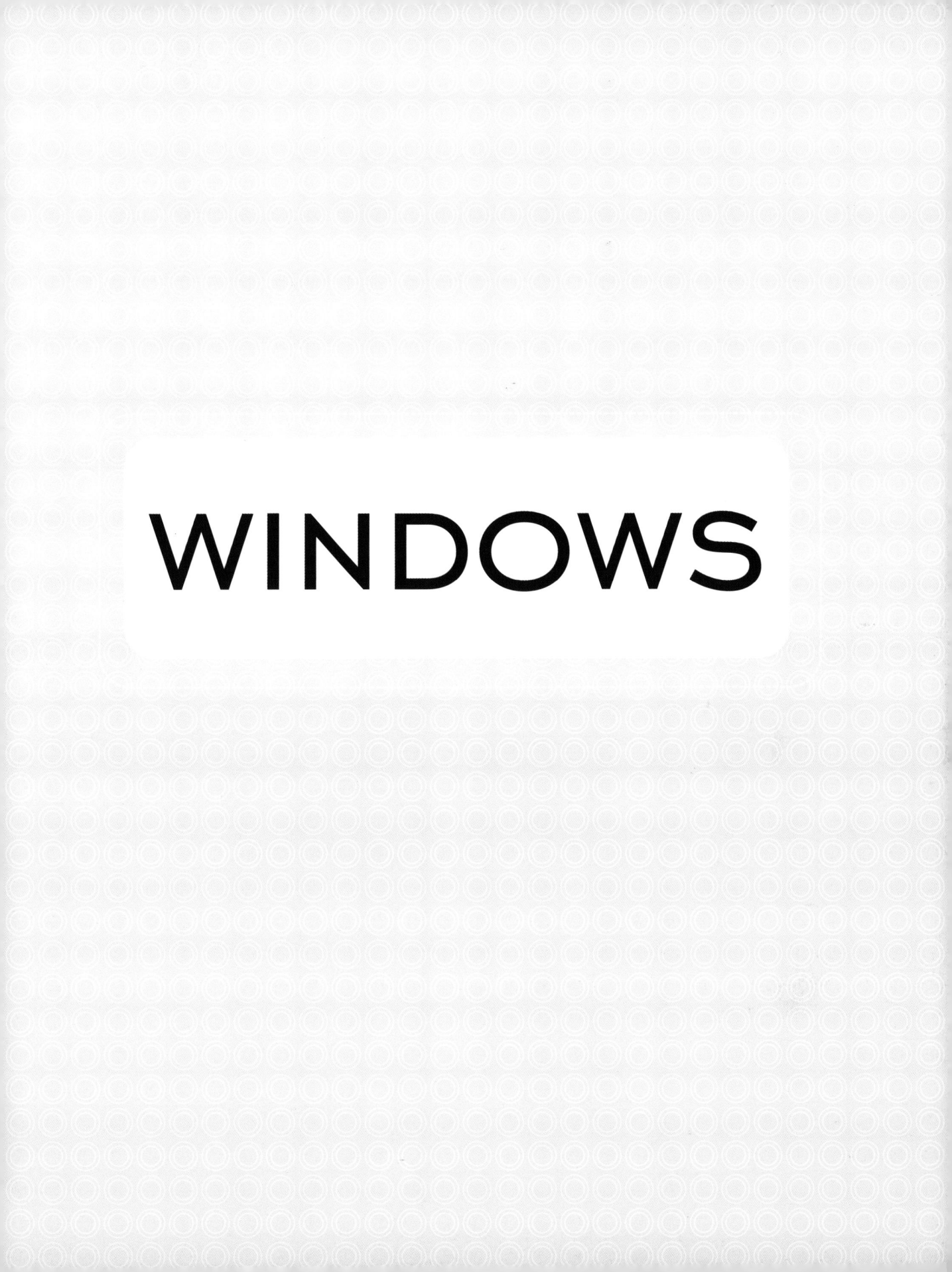

WINDOWS

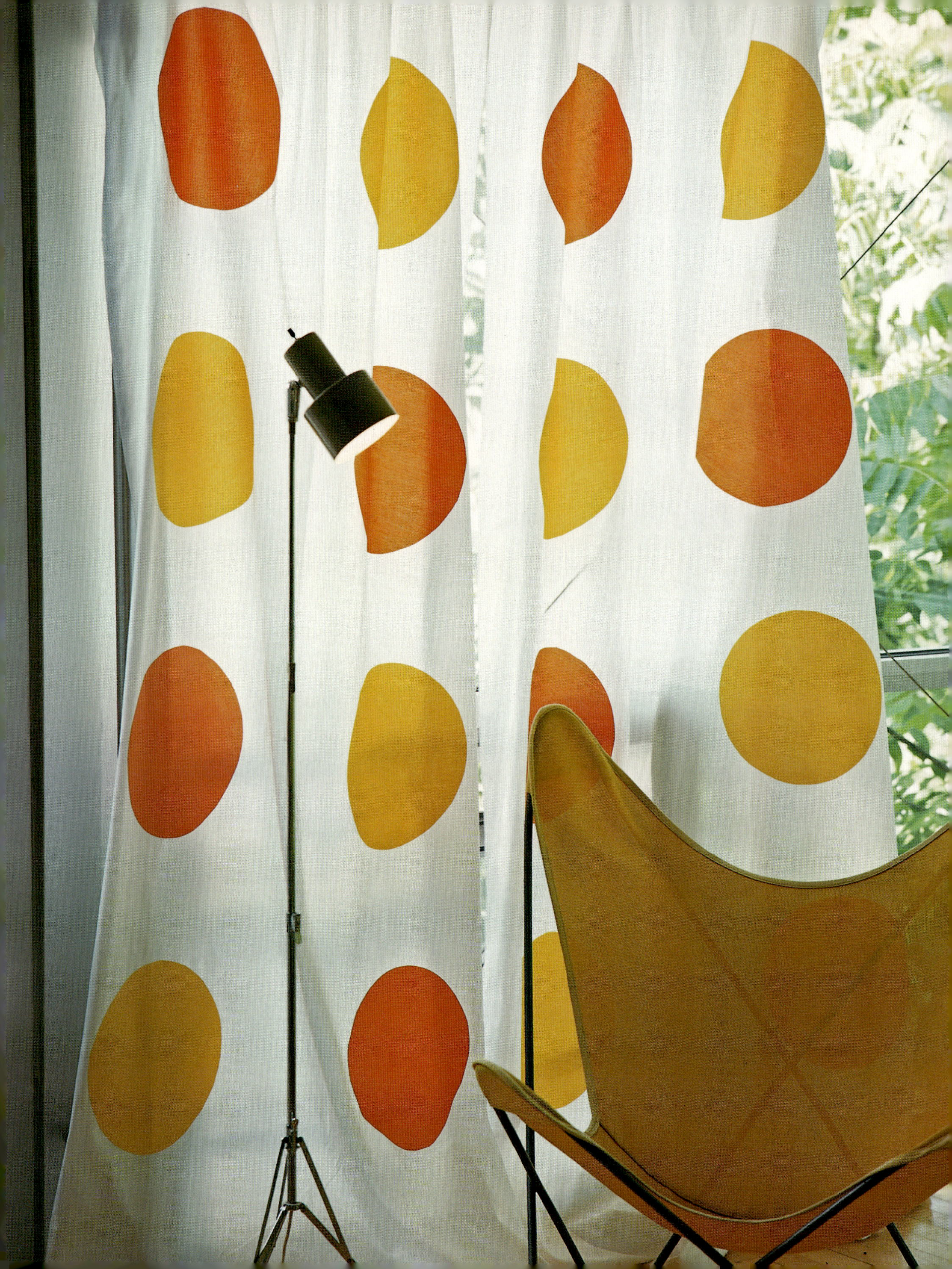

WINDOWS

polka-dot appliqué panels

Large-scale fabric patterns, such as those by Marimekko, are hard to find and expensive. But you can design your own multicolor textiles using homemade iron-ons. These floor-length curtains are made of broadcloth, a cotton that comes in many colors and is one of the cheapest fabrics available. Fusible webbing allows you to make an appliqué in any shape you want. I used the entire width of white fabric (the standard forty-five inches) and left the edges as they were on the bolt. If you cut a smaller width, make fused hems on these edges too.

5 yards white broadcloth
1 yard each orange and yellow broadcloth
Scissors
L-shaped ruler
Pencil
Towel
Iron
Tape measure
Straight pins
Iron-on seam tape
4 yards paper-backed fusible webbing
Dinner plate
Washcloth
Curtain rod and mounting hardware

1. Wash and dry the three fabrics. Fold the white fabric exactly in half widthwise and cut along the fold to get two equal panels. Use the L-shaped ruler and pencil to ensure that your cut creates 90-degree angles.

2. Place the towel over your work area to create a large ironing surface. Set the iron on high heat. At one end of each panel (the rod end), make a 3-inch fold and secure it with pins. At the other end of each panel, make and pin a 1-inch hem. Iron the hems to make the folds crisp, then remove the pins.

3. Adjust your iron temperature according to the instructions of your seam tape. Cut four lengths of tape equal to the width of each panel. Place the tape inside the fold of a hem, then iron to melt the adhesive and fuse the fold shut. Repeat with the remaining three hems.

WINDOWS

4. Adjust your iron temperature according to the instructions of your fusible webbing. Cover the orange and yellow fabrics with abutting strips of webbing. Iron the webbing gently until it adheres, smoothing out any wrinkles.

5. Put the plate on the webbing-backed fabric and trace around it, drawing eight circles per color. Cut out the circles.

6. Lay out a curtain panel on your work surface. Do some math to figure out equal placement for your polka dots. Make a light pencil mark for the center of each dot, and repeat on the other panel.

7. If your webbing's instructions call for a pressing cloth, dampen the washcloth. Peel the paper backing off your first dot. Center it over a pencil mark, then iron it on, with the washcloth on top, so that it adheres completely and looks smooth. Repeat with the remaining dots, alternating the colors.

8. Attach the curtain rod to the window frame and hang the panels.

studded plum sheer

WINDOWS

The fabric glues and iron-on tapes so indispensable for no-sew curtain making don't work on gauzy fabrics, so metal studs hold everything together in this project. Studding the panel is a time sucker, but the result is well worth it. (In the tedium of gentle hammering, I pondered whether a halfway-covered sheer would look all right.) The purple creates a cool ambience when the sun shines through, and the fluttering squares add visual interest any time of day. If you don't live in mosquito country like I do, open up the window and let this baby blow.

Tape measure
Purple organza or other sheer fabric (see step 1 for determining the yardage)
Rotary cutter
Self-healing cutting mat with a measuring grid
L-shaped ruler

Pencil
Straight pins
Iron and ironing board
Metal studs for fabric
Hammer
Straightedge
Tension rod to fit inside your window

1. Measure the length of the inside of your window frame. Double the number to determine the amount of organza to buy.

2. Use the rotary cutter and mat to cut out a fabric panel that is the length of your window, plus 4 inches for hems. Use the L-shaped ruler and pencil to make sure you cut 90-degree angles.

3. Pin a 1-inch hem along each vertical side of the panel. Iron the hems to make the folds crisp. Pin a 3-inch hem along the top edge and a 1-inch hem along the bottom, and press these with the iron.

4. Working on a clean surface, place the sheer panel right side up (with the raw edges of the hems on the underside). Place the teeth of a stud through the fabric near one end of the 3-inch hem, about 1 inch up from the hem's raw edge and also penetrating the side hem. Hold the stud in place and flip

over the fabric so that the stud's teeth are pointed up. Use your thumb and first finger to keep the fabric down over the teeth while you hammer gently. They should flatten out and fasten the layers of fabric together.

5. Repeat step 4 on the opposite edge of the 3-inch hem, then attach more studs at an equal distance from one another along the entire length of the large hem. A 2- or 3-inch spacing pattern provides enough support.

6. Secure the bottom hem with studs, using the same spacing pattern established in step 5.

7. Cut pieces of the remaining fabric to the size of your cutting mat. Place a fabric piece over the mat, put the straightedge over the fabric, and follow the measurements on the mat to cut out 2-inch strips. Next cut the strips into 2-inch squares.

8. Lay out your first row of squares on the sheer below the 3-inch hem in a desired pattern. Pin each square in place near its edge, not through its center. Hammer a stud through the center of each square and remove pins.

9. Place the next row of squares even with the first. Pin and attach the studs. Continue in this way until you cover the sheer with squares.

10. Secure the side hems with evenly placed studs. Since these hems don't carry weight, you can space the studs around every 6 inches.

11. Remove all pins, insert the tension rod in the 3-inch hem, and hang your sheer.

If you want to trade a little extra dinero for faster results, buy a stud-setting machine and forget hammering. It's like a big girlie stapler made for fastening studs, rhinestones, and other toothy jewels to fabric.

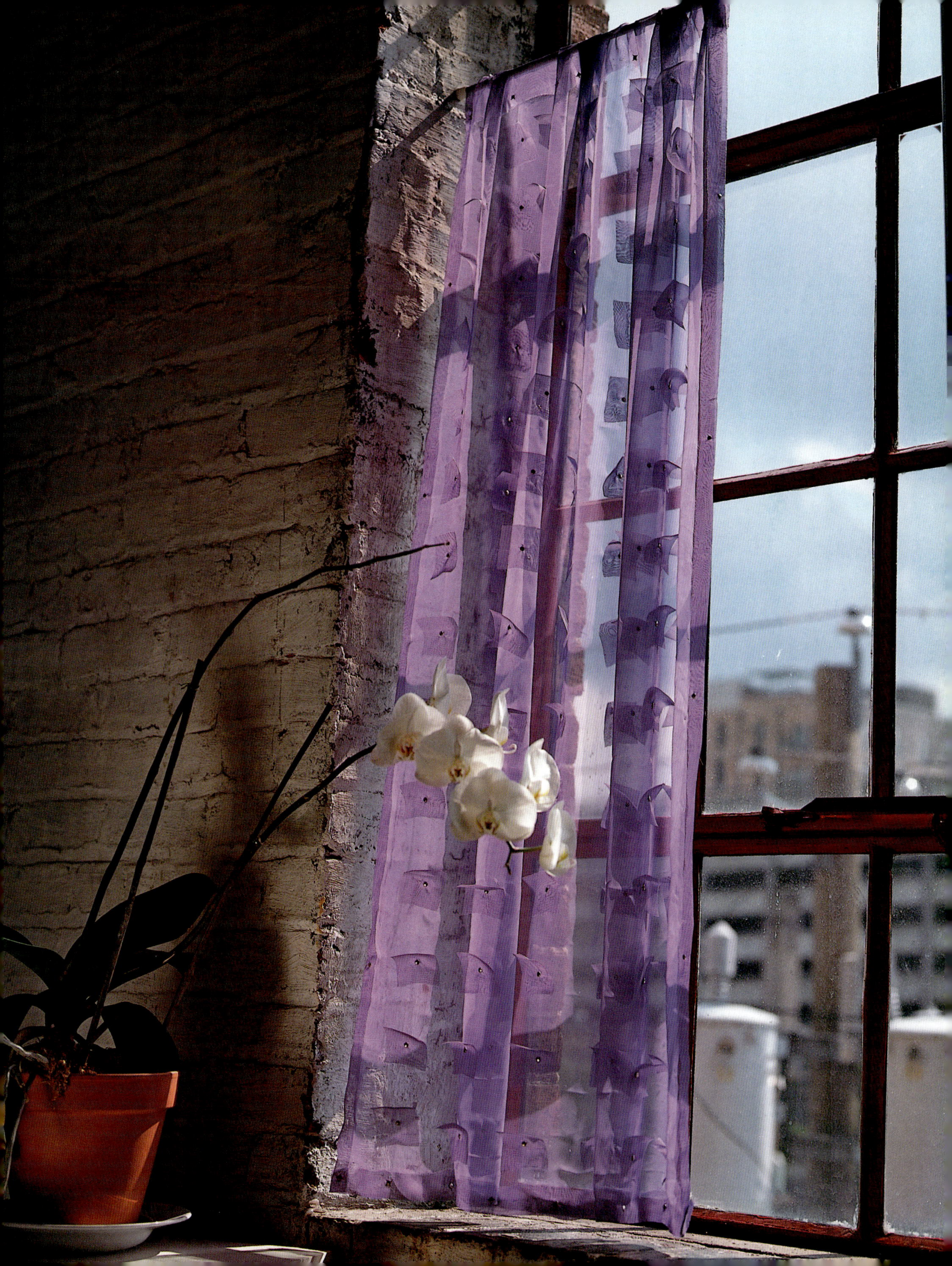

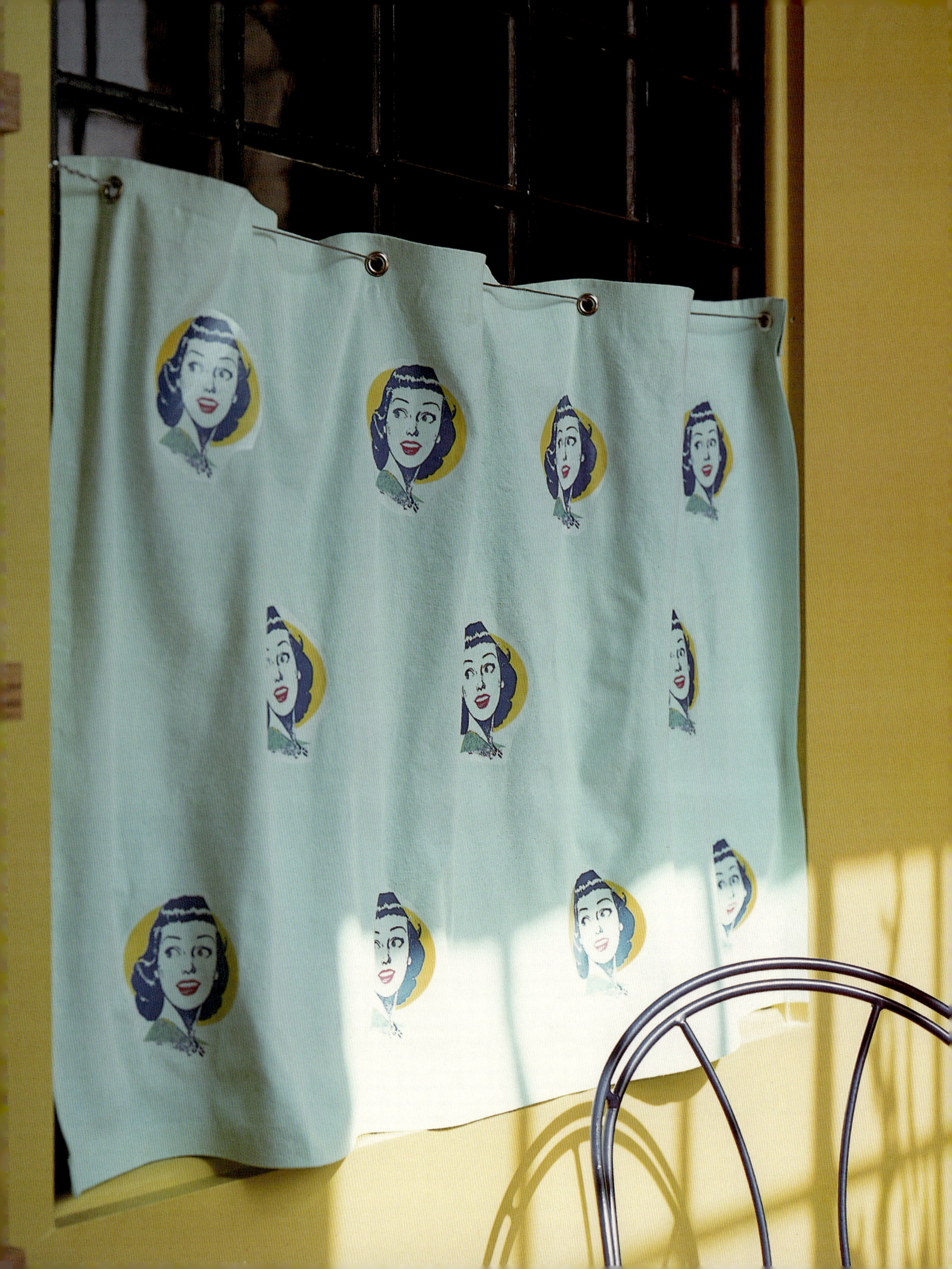

WINDOWS

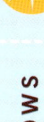

clip-art café curtain

This curtain is great in a kitchen or dining room, since it covers only half the window and has a cozy restaurant feel. I chose a fifties icon for my decoration, but the glut of free and cheap clip art on the Internet leaves your options wide open. Print your chosen image onto transfer paper and fuse it to your fabric for the nostalgic look of a vintage textile.

Tape measure
Cotton duck fabric (see step 1 for determining the yardage)
Scissors
L-shaped ruler
Pencil
Straight pins
Iron and ironing board
Iron-on seam tape

Color printer
Clip art
Iron-on transfer paper (available in the clothing-decorating section of craft stores)
$1/2$-inch silver-tone grommets
Grommet pliers
2 small screw eyes
Picture wire

1. Measure the length and width of the inside of your window frame. Divide the length in half and add 3 inches to determine the amount of fabric to buy. When you're ready to cut out the panel, add 25 percent to the window's width to allow for pleats and hems. Use the L-shaped ruler and pencil to make sure you cut at 90-degree angles.

2. Pin 1-inch hems along the vertical edges of the panel. Iron the hems to make the folds crisp, then remove the pins. Adjust your iron temperature according to the instructions of your seam tape. Cut two lengths of tape equal to the length of each panel. Place the tape inside the fold of a hem, then iron to melt the adhesive and fuse the fold shut.

WINDOWS

3. Pin a 1-inch hem along the bottom edge and a 2-inch hem along the top. Iron, remove the pins, and fuse with the seam tape.

4. Print out your clip art, as many copies as needed, on the transfer paper. (Keep in mind that the image will be backward once you apply it to the fabric.) Cut out the images, removing all the excess paper around the ink. Arrange the cutouts, ink side down, in offset rows on the curtain and pin them in place. Iron them on according to the paper manufacturer's instructions.

5. Place the grommets 6 to 8 inches apart along the 2-inch hem. Make Xs with the pencil inside each grommet to mark the place where you need to cut an opening. Make the holes with the grommet pliers or scissors.

6. Place the stem of a grommet through the front side of a hole and place a ring around the stem on the backside. Use the grommet pliers to bend the stem over the ring. Repeat for all the grommets.

7. Attach the screw eyes at opposite sides of the window frame at the height you want the curtain to hang. Put one end of the picture wire through a screw eye and twist to secure it. Thread the curtain onto the wire. Pull the loose end of the wire as taut as you can, insert it in the other screw eye, and twist to secure. Clip off any excess wire with scissors.

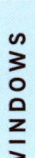

upholstered cardboard valance

WINDOWS

Sometimes a window needs thick drapes that keep out the light, and sometimes it just needs an inobtrusive accessory to tie it in with the rest of the space. This plush window topper has a piece of cardboard as its base, but it's so sturdy and attractive that your friends will never know you went Dumpster diving for boxes.

Curtain rod with curved ends and mounting hardware
Tape measure
Piece of cardboard at least 10 inches tall and as wide as your window, plus at least 8 inches
Pencil
Long ruler
Utility knife
At least 5 twist ties
Quilt batting
Scissors
Hot glue gun and glue sticks
1/2 yard upholstery fabric (Most upholstery fabrics are 60 inches wide. If your window is wider than 52 inches, buy additional yardage and use the fabric lengthwise.)

1. Mount the curtain rod with its ends outside the window frame. Measure the width of the mounted rod, including the curved portions.

2. On the cardboard, use the pencil and ruler to draw a rectangle with the width determined above and a height of 10 inches. Cut it out with the utility knife. Draw lines on the rectangle to mark where the board will bend around the rod ends, score the lines, and gently coax the board to flex.

3. Five inches from the top of the board, mark a spot at the midpoint, one near either edge, and at least two other spots between these. If your cardboard has bends besides the ones you made, mark a spot on each of these. Use the tip of the knife to make vertical pairs of small holes at each mark. Insert the ends of the twist ties into the holes from behind and give them a couple of twists to hold them in place for now. (See figure 2.)

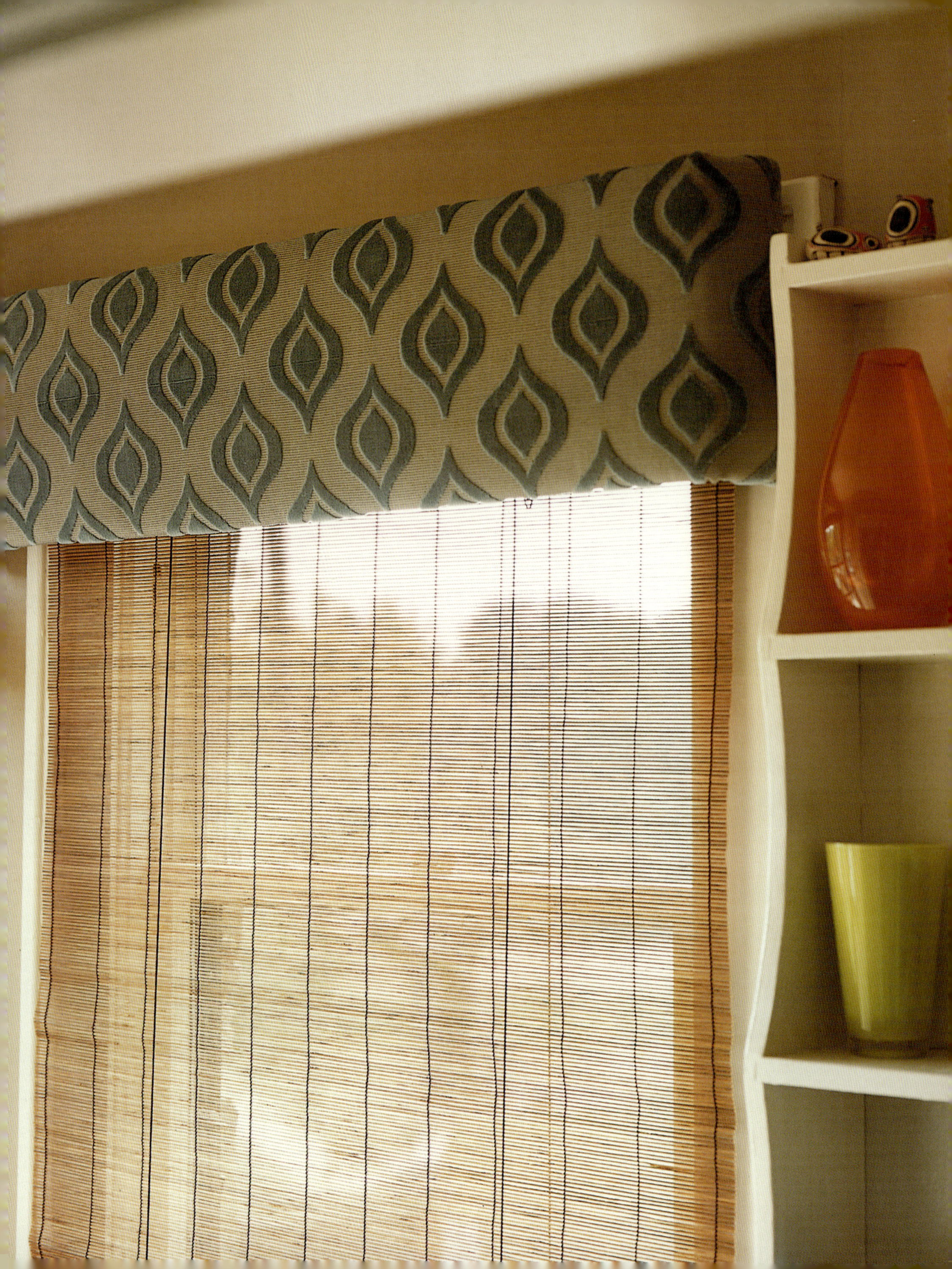

WINDOWS

4. Place the board, twist-tie ends up, on a double layer of quilt batting. Cut the batting along the shape of the board, leaving about 1 inch of space all around. Put hot glue on the batting edges and press them down onto the board. The glue will also fuse the two layers of batting.

5. Place the board on top of the wrong-side-up fabric. Cut the fabric along the shape of the board, leaving about 3 inches of space all around. Beginning in the middle of the board, pull the fabric taut on either side and glue it to the board.

6. Starting with the ends, hang the valance by twisting the ties around the curtain rod.

Figure 2

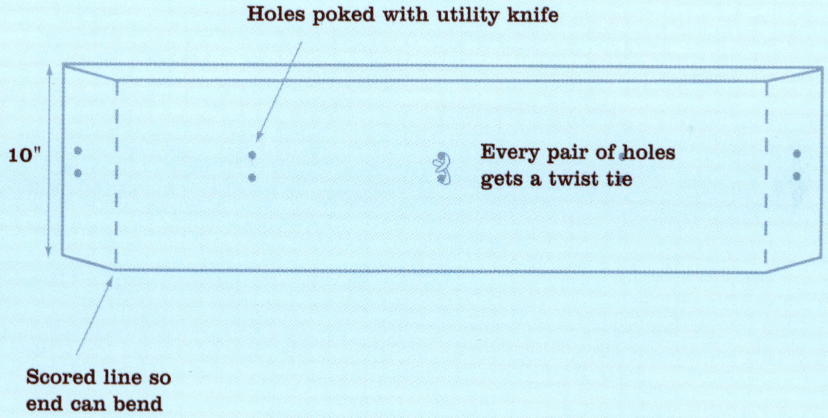

Holes poked with utility knife

10"

Every pair of holes gets a twist tie

Scored line so end can bend

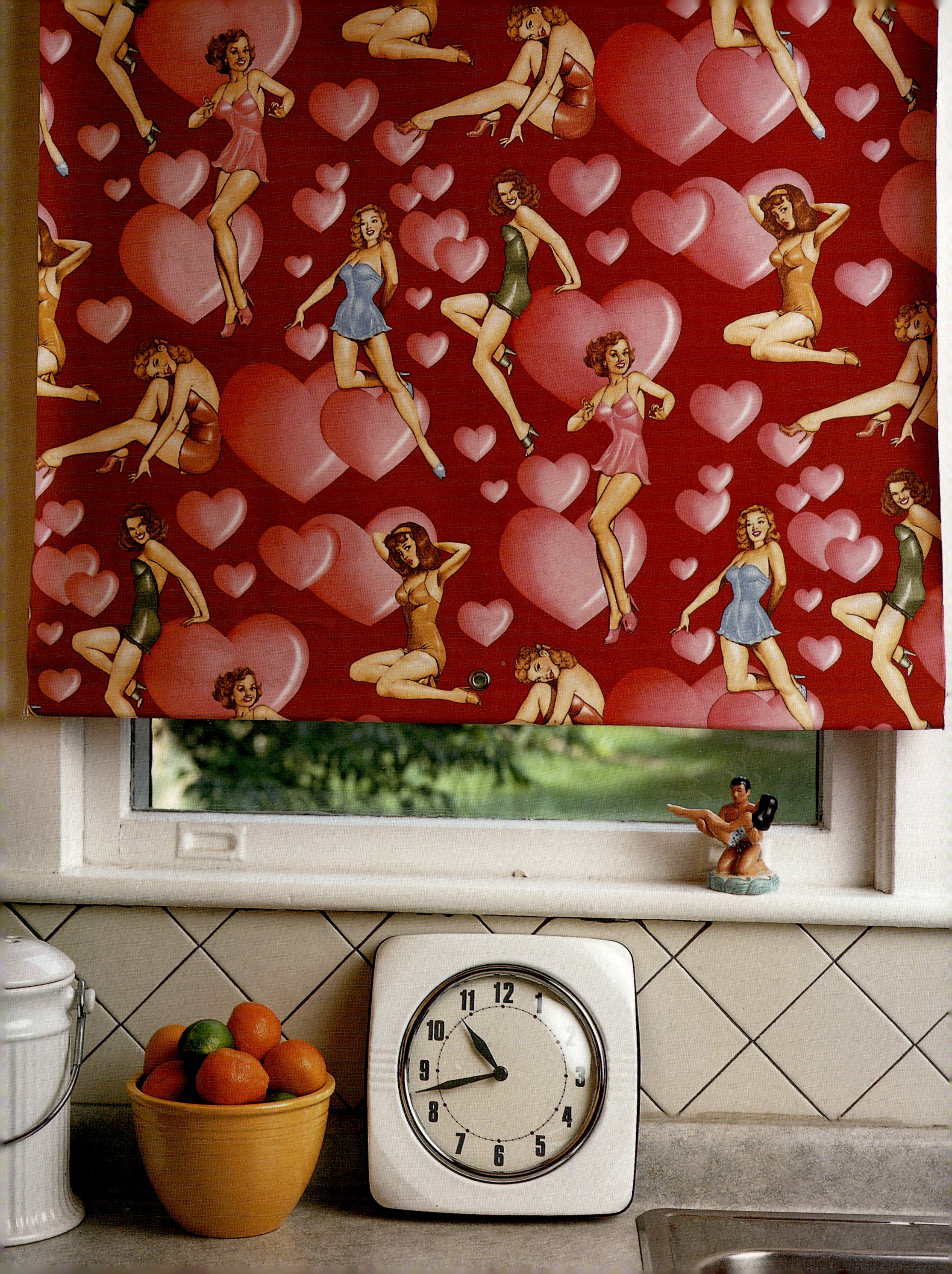

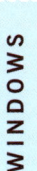

fabric-covered roller shade

WINDOWS

Vinyl shades epitomize cheap window coverage, but you can festoon them with great fabric. I don't usually go for themed prints, but I couldn't resist this one adorned with large-scale bathing beauties from yesteryear. The suggestive shade is perfect for a girlie powder room or kitschy kitchen.

Scissors
Lightweight opaque fabric (enough to cover the length of your window, plus 1 foot)
Tape measure
Vinyl roller shade
Foam brush
Decoupage medium
Cardboard scrap (optional)
Rotary cutter
Self-healing cutting mat

1. Cut the fabric a few inches wider than the adjusted width of the shade.

2. Unroll the shade and lay it right side up on a clean floor or table. Flip up the bottom 3 inches so that the backside is exposed, and brush this area with decoupage medium. Place the end of the fabric panel over the glue, right side up, centering the width. Smooth it down, using the cardboard as a tool, if desired. Let dry for a few minutes.

3. Flip the shade bottom back down and bunch up the fabric below the shade. Brush decoupage medium onto the bottom third of the front of the shade, then smooth the fabric over the glue, pushing toward the top and sides. Quickly work out any wrinkles or bubbles. Let this area dry for a few minutes, then continue in this way until the front of the shade is covered.

4. Flip the shade over and brush decoupage medium on the excess fabric closest to the shade sides. The glue will keep the edges from fraying. Once the glue is dry, use the rotary cutter and mat to cut the fabric even with the shade sides. Trim any stray threads. Hang the shade.

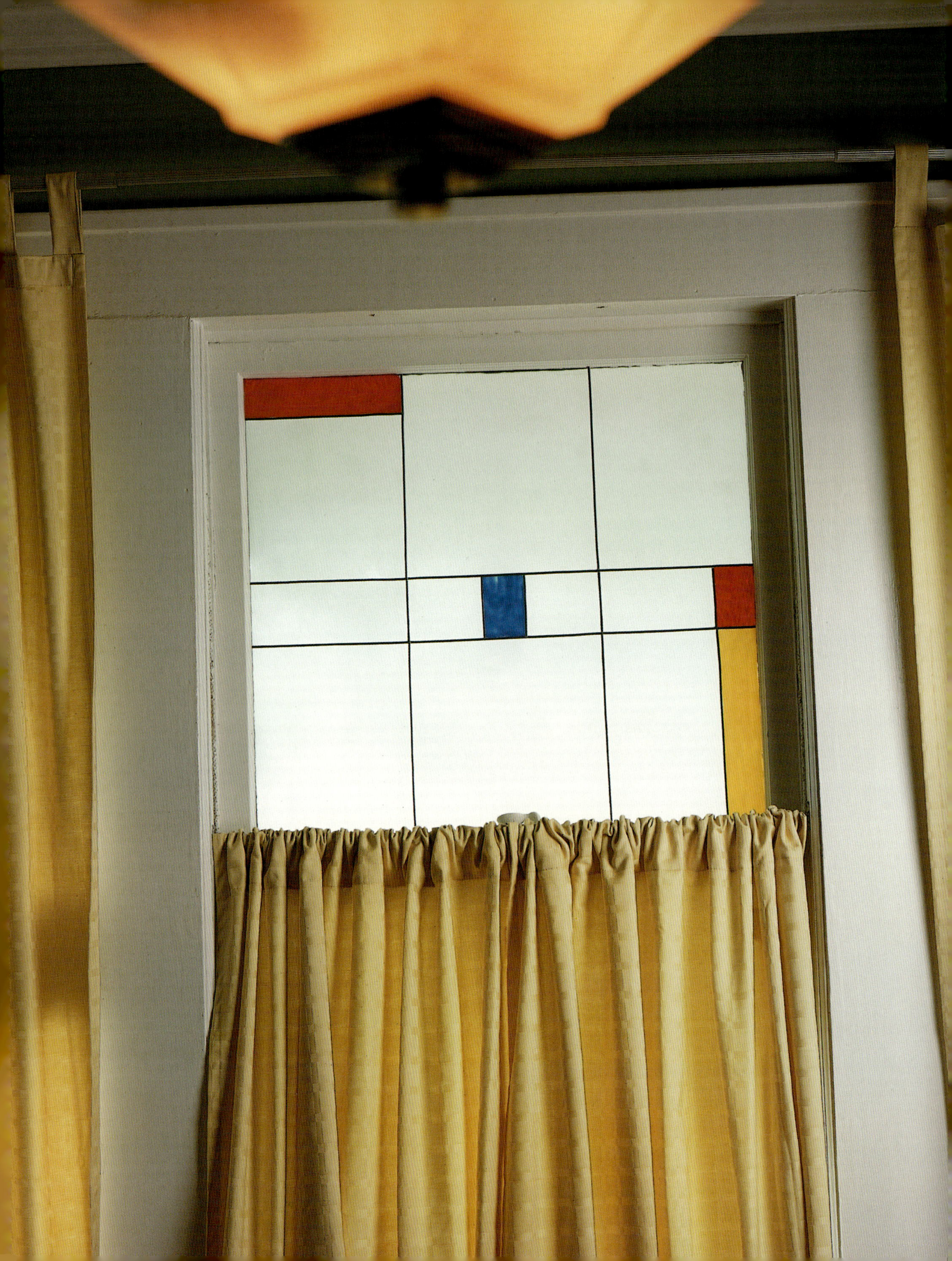

WINDOWS

mondrian "stained-glass" window

Block a blah view or simply bring color to a window without the froufrou of curtains. My abstract pattern is inspired by the paintings of Piet Mondrian, who made a living with romantic landscapes and floral portraits but today is best known for his white canvases with blocks of primary colors.

Tape measure
Pencil
Graph paper
Adhesive-backed leading lines
Self-healing cutting mat
Craft knife
Masking tape
Envelope

Scrap paper
Ruler
Template plastic
Gel-type glass paints (such as Plaid Gallery Glass Window Color) in red, yellow, and blue
Glass-frosting spray

1. Measure your windowpanes. Draw your design to these dimensions on graph paper and note the size and color of each shape.

2. Make pencil marks on the window frame to indicate where you'll start each leading line. Cut the lines to size on the mat using the craft knife. To place the lines at right angles, tape the envelope to the glass as a guide.

3. Measure inside the areas where you will place the color blocks (the actual measurements may differ from those you planned on paper). Write down the sizes you need for each paint color, then draw a template on scrap paper for each size.

4. Put the scrap paper drawings under the sheets of template plastic and use the lines as a guide for putting down masking tape on the plastic.

WINDOWS

5. Paint inside the masking tape. Squeeze a generous amount of the gel paint in concentric rows—don't use a paintbrush. After a masked area is filled with paint, use the bottle's tip to swirl together the rows and even out the texture. Let the paint dry for 48 hours, or as long as recommended by the manufacturer.

6. Use the ruler and craft knife to make clean edges on the color blocks, which will now feel like fruit leather. Gently peel them off the plastic. Place them on the window between the designated leading lines. Retrim the color blocks or adjust the leading lines as needed to make them butt nicely.

7. Apply three coats of glass-frosting spray to make the blank areas appear white. Let the spray dry between coats.

When you're ready to see your old window again, simply peel off the leading lines and color blocks. The latter can be used again. Scrub off the frosting with nail polish remover and paper towels or scrape it off with a razor.

lightbulb curtain finials

WINDOWS

Kick your store-bought curtain rods and finials curbside. They're expensive underachievers that can't compete with drapery hardware that *lights up*. That's right, not only are these bulb finials pretty baubles, they also function as Mr. Edison intended. Plug them in to cast a soft glow over your evening shenanigans.

Curtain brackets with hardware
Tape measure
Pencil
Piece of 3/4-inch EMT conduit (see step 2 for length)
Pipe cutter
Hand drill with 1/4-inch bit made for metal
Small metal file
Curtains
Two 12-foot lengths of lamp wire (or more if you don't have an electrical outlet below your window)
2 replacement plugs
Scissors or wire strippers
2 candelabra sockets
Screwdriver
Rubber bands (optional)
2 candelabra lightbulbs

1. Mount the brackets just outside the window frame.

2. With a tape measure and pencil, mark your window frame's width plus 4 inches onto the conduit. Cut using the pipe cutter.

3. Put your foot on the conduit to anchor it and drill a 1/4-inch hole 1 1/2 inches in from one end. Use the file to get rid of any sharp bits. Repeat at the other end. Put the curtains on the rod and push them toward the center.

4. Attach one end of each lamp wire to a replacement plug. Slide each opposite end through a drilled hole and out the near end of the conduit. Use the scissors or wire strippers to remove 1 inch of insulation from wires.

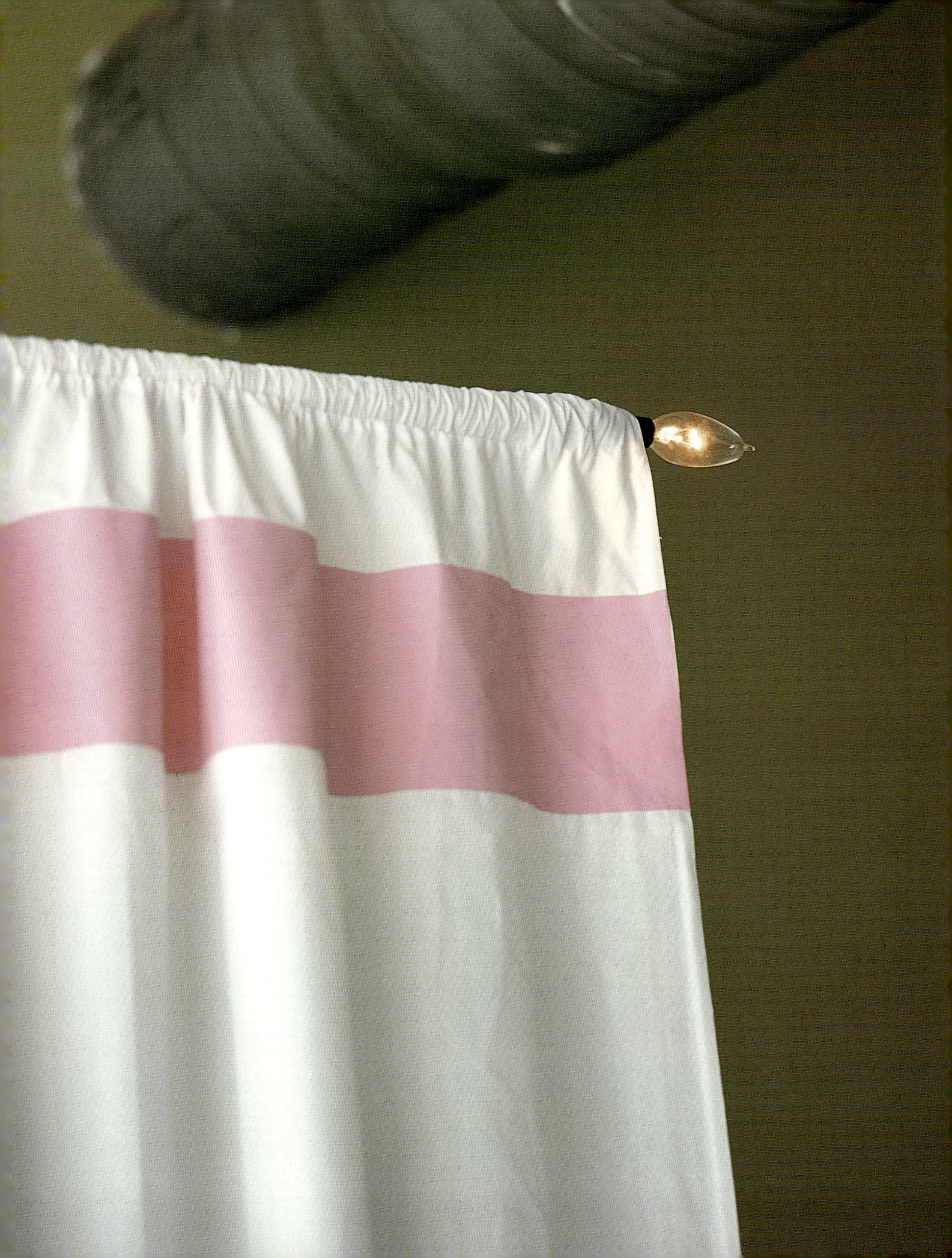

WINDOWS

5. Slide a socket's cardboard tube over one wire end. Wrap the exposed wires around the appropriate terminal screws of the socket interior. The ribbed wire is neutral and goes to the silver screw, and the smooth wire is hot and goes to the brass screw. If your socket or wires differ, follow the manufacturer's instructions for assembly. Tighten the screws. Slide the cardboard over the socket and insert the socket into the conduit's end. If the fit is not secure, wrap rubber bands around the cardboard then retry. Screw in a bulb. Repeat this step at the other end of the conduit.

6. Plug your bulbs into a nearby outlet. Hide the lamp wires behind the curtains.

Conduit comes in ten-foot lengths, and you can link them with straight or L-shaped connectors to make continuous, dramatic window treatments.

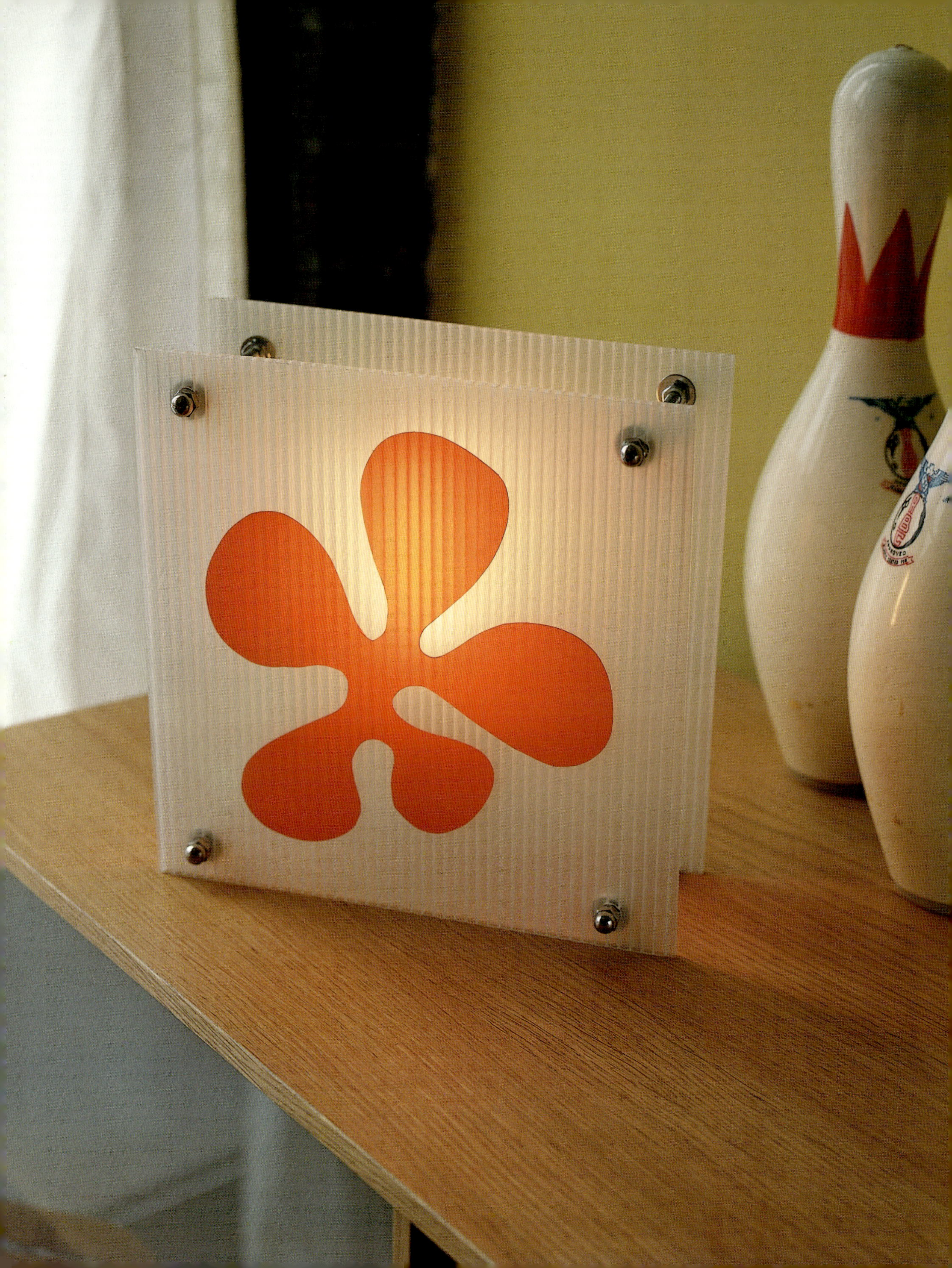

LIGHTING

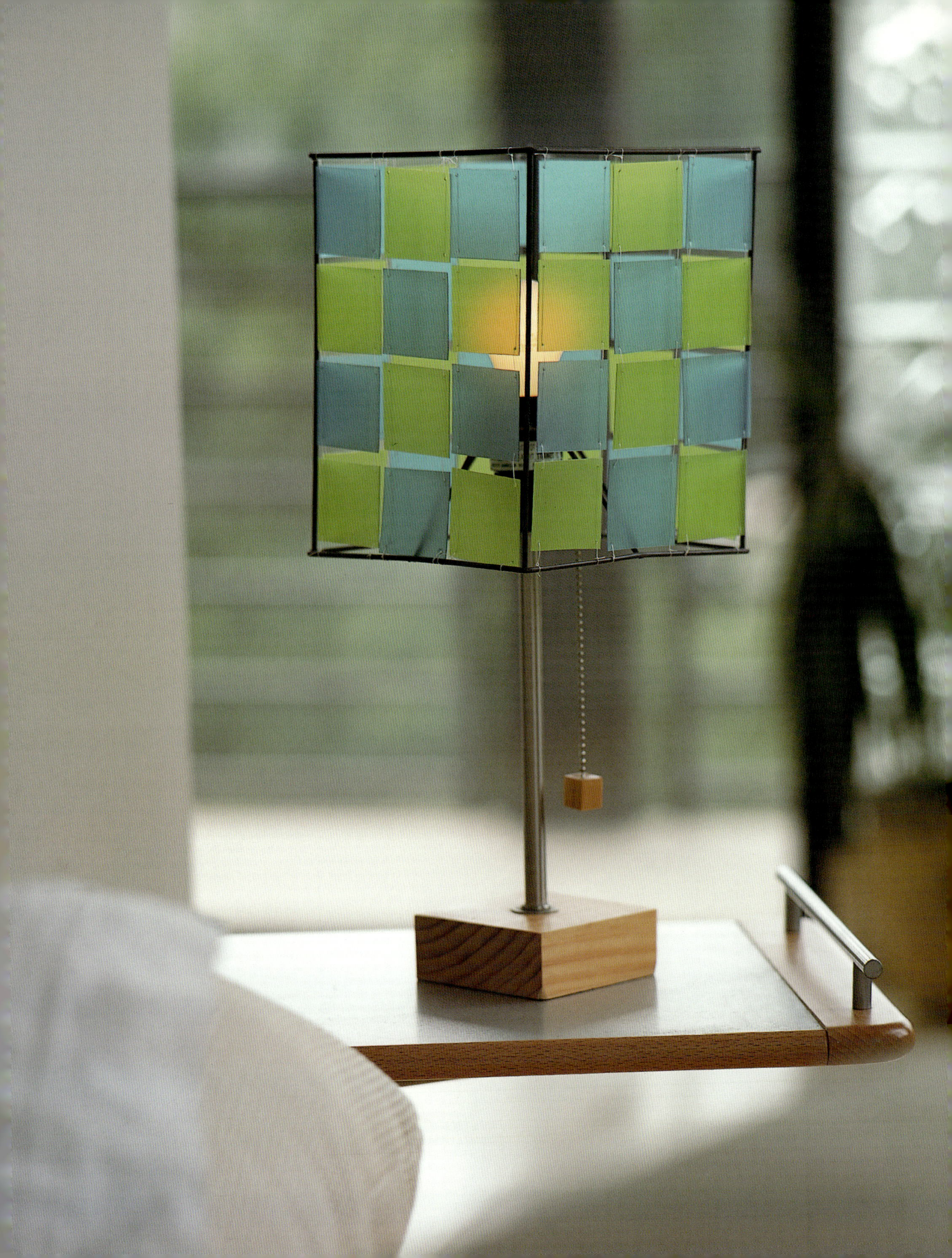

LIGHTING

plastic mosaic lamp shade

Bright-colored plastic folders make for an inexpensive shade that filters light beautifully, especially at night, sending brilliant squares all over your walls. Instead of a checkerboard look, you can experiment with stripes or an asymmetrical pattern. You can also adapt the measurements easily for lamp shades of different shapes and sizes. The most difficult part about this project is keeping your dignity in the office supply store while you ravage the portfolio aisle, looking for the coolest plastics.

$6^{1}/_{2}$ x 8-inch rectangular lamp shade
Utility knife
Self-healing cutting mat
Ruler
Frosted plastic folders in two coordinating colors
Phone book or another soft surface for punching
Awl
Thick sewing needle
Scissors
Clear nylon beading cord

1. Strip off the lamp shade's covering, leaving the frame only.

2. With the utility knife, mat, and ruler, cut the folders into 2-inch strips, then cut the strips into 1-inch sections. You may have to score the lines two or more times before you get a clean break. Make 24 plastic rectangles in each color.

3. Using the phone book as a work surface, punch a hole in each corner of each rectangle with the awl. If any holes are too small for the beading cord to fit through, enlarge them gently with the needle. The key to keeping the rectangles from sliding down the cord freely is making holes that fit snugly around the cord, so don't make the holes too large.

4. Cut 24 pieces of cord 12 inches long. Make your first strip of rectangles by threading two cords by hand through the holes of four rectangles, alternating the colors. The 2-inch edges of the rectangles should be vertical. Run the cord

LIGHTING

behind the plastic so it's less obvious. Use a double knot to tie the top and bottom of the two cords onto the top and bottom of the lamp shade frame.

5. Continue threading groups of four rectangles and tying them onto the frame until the shade is complete. Arrange the rectangles so they're evenly spaced, then trim the ends of the cord.

LIGHTING

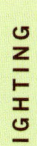

art paper tube shade

Shabby accent lamps abound at thrift stores and, shamefully, on our own bedside tables. You can redeem the ugliest luminaire with this cylindrical shade that slips over the whole thing. The look is completely versatile, because it depends on which art paper you choose.

Pruning shears
1/4 x 1/4 x 36-inch balsa-wood strip (available in the woodworking section of craft stores)
Long ruler
Three 8-inch wood embroidery hoops
Hot glue gun and glue sticks
20 x 27-inch piece of art paper
Pencil
Scissors
Craft knife
Small lamp

1. Use the pruning shears to cut two 17-inch pieces from the soft balsa strip. Remove the inner circles from the embroidery hoops and discard the outer circles. Make a frame with the hoops and balsa-wood strips by gluing the strips inside the hoops. The sticks should be across from each other, and the hoops should be at both ends and in the middle.

2. Put the paper wrong side up on a clean, smooth surface. Place the frame on its side along the short edge of the paper, centering it. Make pencil marks on either side of each hoop. Remove the frame and put a dab of glue inside these three marks. Reposition the frame in the glue (the strips should be on the sides, not on the top or bottom of the tube) and hold it until the glue sets. (See figure 3.)

3. Working up from the paper, put a few inches of glue along the outside of each hoop, then roll the frame forward. Hold it in place until the glue sets.

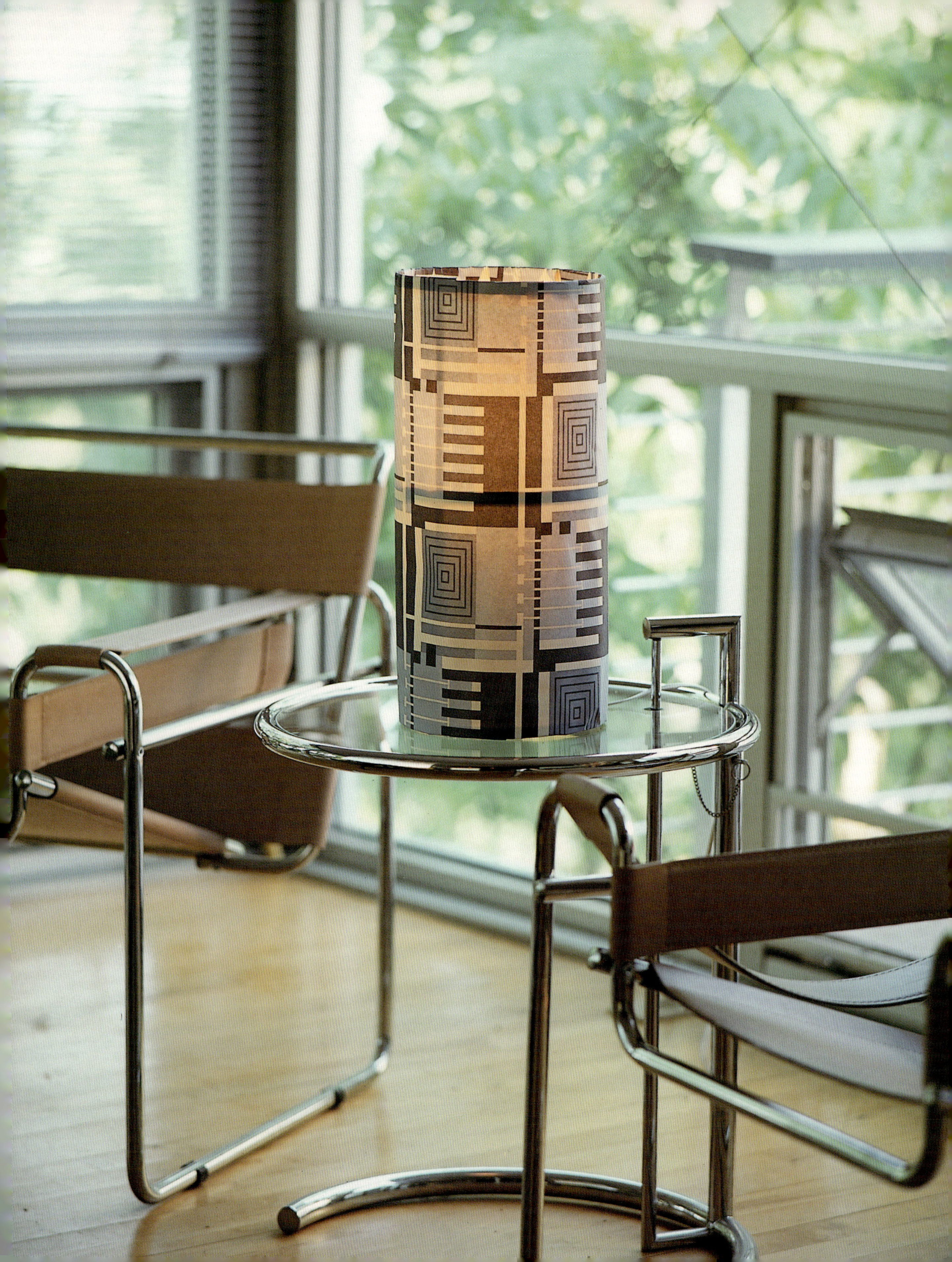

Repeat until you reach the paper's end. Glue one paper edge over the other to close the seam.

4. Place the shade upright and cut a triangle every inch or so in the excess paper on the end to help it fold down. Put glue on the inside of the end hoop one section at a time, then fold down the paper and hold it until the glue sets. Repeat on the other end of the shade.

5. Choose one end for the bottom and use the craft knife to cut an X along the paper's seam, just above the bottom hoop, for the lamp's cord to pass through. Put the cord through the X and place the shadeless lamp inside the tube shade.

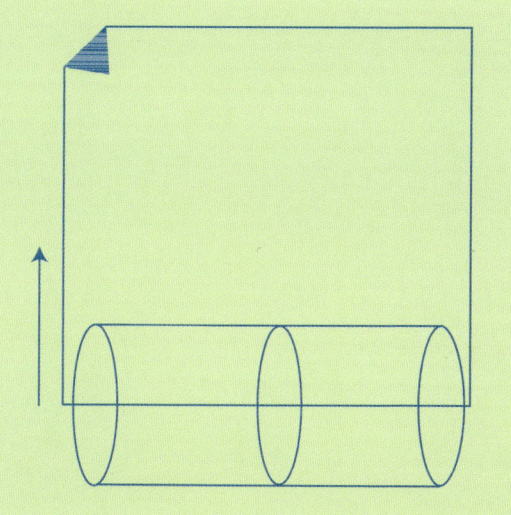

Figure 3

Place glue on the hoops a few inches at a time and roll the frame forward.

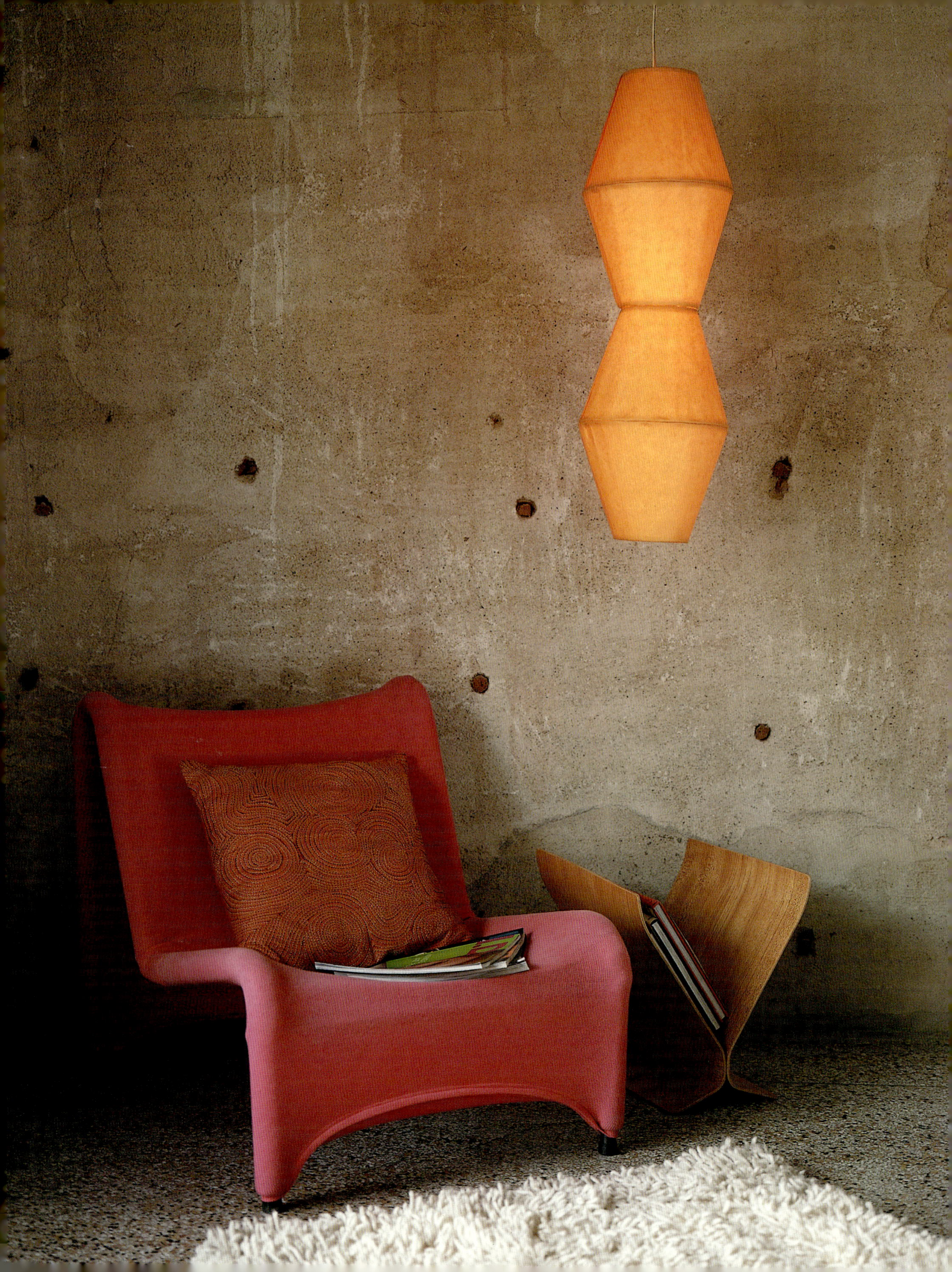

LIGHTING

stacked shade lantern

One lamp shade gets a yawn, but in multiples these decor staples become sculptural. Use six or even more shades for a larger-scale creation, or assemble them in twos and make table lamps or pendant lights. You can use your purchased shades as they are or add a translucent paper with random flecks or a subtle pattern to create interest when light shines through. A holiday rope light provides the rays, so you don't have to mess with electrical wiring.

Wire cutters
Four 8-inch-tall, light-colored lamp shades with ring-type shade holders
4 sheets art paper
Pencil
Ruler
Scissors
Double-sided tape
White glue

String
Two $1/8$-IP hex nuts (IP stands for "iron pipe," the standard measurement of lighting parts)
30-inch $1/8$-IP threaded rod
Rope light
Extension cord
Screw hook

1. With the wire cutters, cut off the shade holder on three of the lamp shades.

2. To cut out art paper for covering the shades, put a shade on its side on top of a sheet of art paper. Start with the shade's seam down. Put a pencil in front of the seam at the top opening and roll the shade, moving the pencil along until the seam touches the paper again. Keep the shade in place, move the pencil to the bottom opening, and roll and trace in the opposite direction. Use the ruler to draw connecting lines between the ends of the parallel curves. Cut out the U shape, but stay about $1/2$ inch outside the lines to allow for seams. (See figure 4.)

LIGHTING

3. To cover each shade, place the paper cutout on a shade so that about 1/2 inch protrudes over both shade openings. Apply double-sided tape where the paper overlaps itself. Cut slits in the excess paper at both openings to help it fold, apply glue to the inside rims of the shade openings, and press down the excess paper.

4. Cut four lengths of string a few feet long and make two Xs on the floor with them. Place one shade, wide end up, in the middle of each X. Put glue on the two shades' rims. Place the remaining shades, wide end down, on top of these shades. Tie the strings at the top of each bundle to hold them together while the glue dries.

5. Untie the bundles. Cut two strings about 6 feet long and make an X on the floor with them. Place one bundle in the middle of the X. Put glue on its rim and place the other bundle on top. The shade with its metal shade holder intact must be either the top or bottom shade, not in the middle. Tie the bundle and let the glue dry. Untie the strings.

6. Put one hex nut about 1 inch from the end of the threaded rod. Place the plug of the rope light just below the nut, then wrap the light snugly around the rod. Pass the end of the rod with the nut through the open end of the lantern. The nut will stop the rod when it reaches the center of the metal shade holder at the opposite end. Place the other nut at the tip of the rod to secure the shade holder.

7. Connect the extension cord to the rope light's plug. Tie the two plugs together with string. Screw the hook into the ceiling. Wrap the extension cord once around the ceiling hook when the lantern is at the correct height, then plug it in.

Figure 4

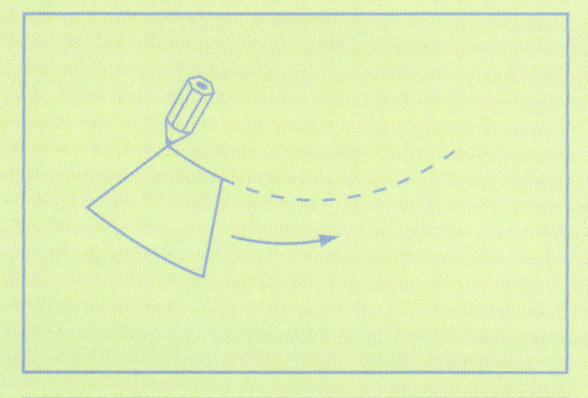

Roll the lamp shade one complete revolution and trace along the top.

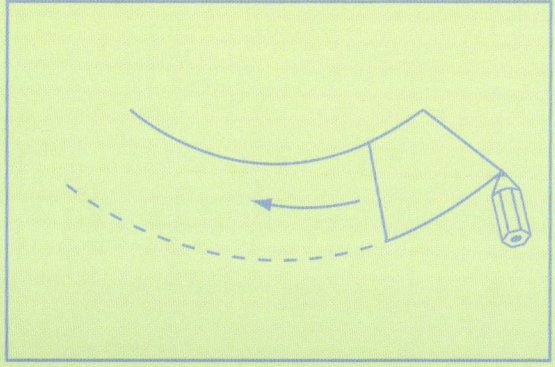

Roll the shade in the other direction and trace along the bottom.

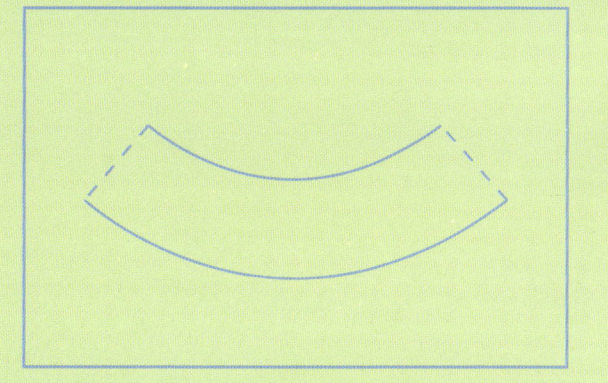

Use a ruler and pencil to connect the two curves, then cut out the U shape.

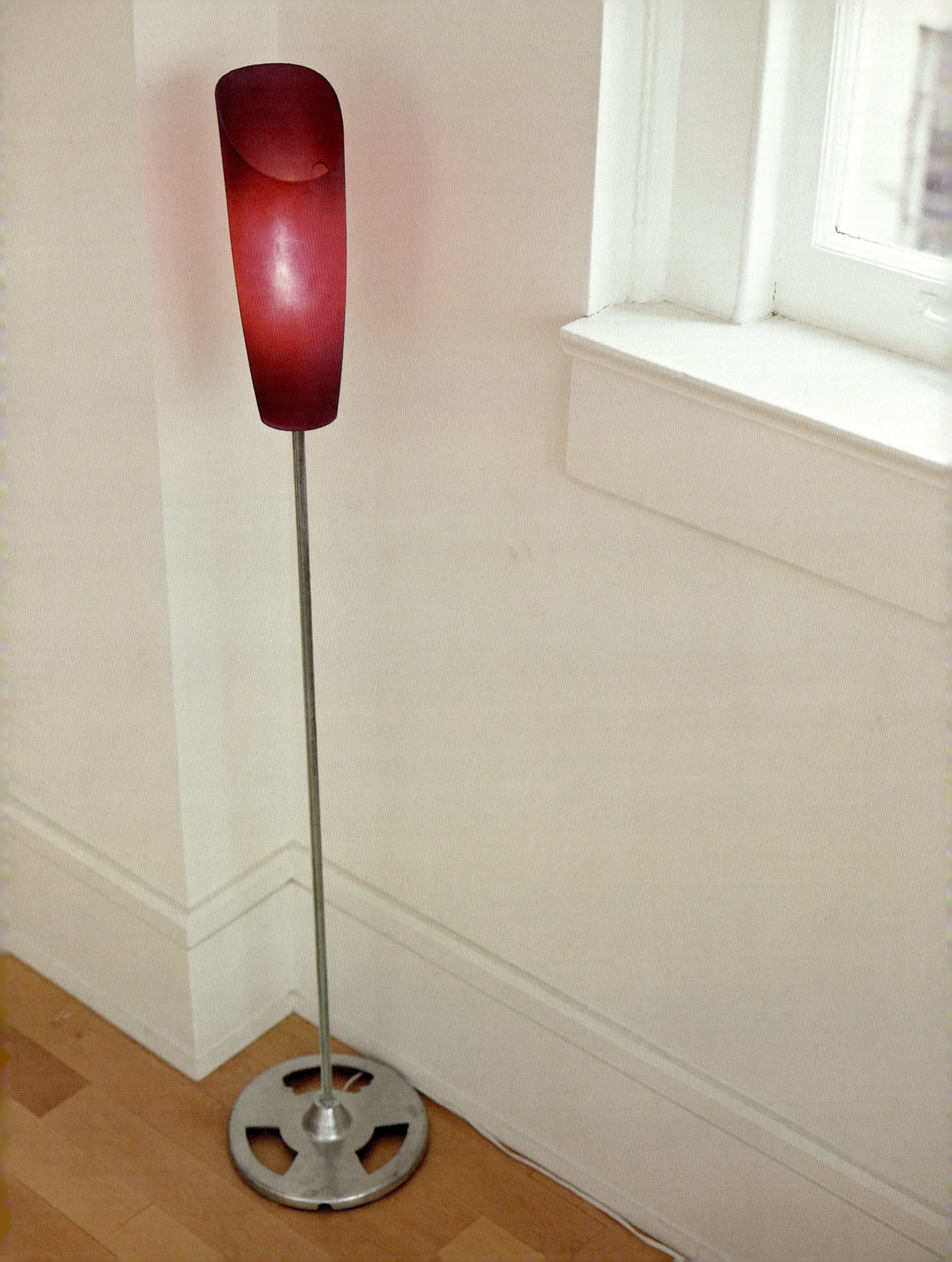

LIGHTING

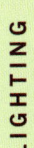

toilet-inspired torchère

Decorating on the cheap knows no bounds—not even your commode's accessories are off limits. The graceful taper of a vaselike toilet brush holder makes it a perfect lamp shade. With a coat of purple frosting and some rays of light shining through, this low-born item will forget its unglamorous past. A wide-mouth plastic bottle with its bottom cut off also makes a good shade. The "naked" look of the iron lamp weight and threaded rod, which usually live inside lamps, not outside, gives an industrial feel.

Hand drill with ½-inch bit
Translucent white toilet brush holder
Newspaper
Purple frosting spray for plastic and glass
Iron lamp weight with ¼-IP center hole (IP stands for "iron pipe," the standard measurement of lighting parts)
Silver spray paint

Four ¼-IP hex nuts
4 washers with ½-inch center holes
¼-IP threaded rod, 36 inches long
Pliers
6-foot lamp wire with plug
¼-IP to ⅛-IP reducer coupling
1-inch ⅛-IP nipple
Lamp socket
Screwdriver
Tubular lightbulb

1. Drill a hole in the bottom center of the toilet brush holder. Rinse off the plastic shavings and dust and dry it off.

2. Outdoors or in a well-ventilated area, cover your work surface with newspaper. Spray the brush holder purple and the lamp weight silver. Let them dry.

3. Put a hex nut, then a washer on one end of the threaded rod and screw it into the top of the weight until about 1 inch protrudes below. Add another washer, then another nut to the protruding end. Tighten the nuts with pliers. Pass the exposed-wire end of the lamp wire through the bottom of the rod and pull it several inches out of the top.

LIGHTING

4. Put a hex nut about 2 inches down from the top of the rod. Place a washer on top, followed by the brush holder. Add another washer and nut to secure the shade.

5. Screw the $1/4$-IP end of the reducer coupling onto the top of the rod, then attach the $1/8$-IP nipple to this. Separate the parts of the lamp socket and screw the socket's end cap to the nipple. Wrap the lamp wires around the appropriate terminal screws of the socket interior (follow the manufacturer's instructions) and tighten the screws. Pull the lamp cord taut from the bottom of the rod, then snap the socket cover in place over the socket interior. Screw in the bulb, plug in the cord, and turn on the lamp.

If it's difficult to get your hand into the torchère to turn this lamp on and off, keep the socket's switch in the on position and plug and unplug the cord.

LIGHTING

amoeba box light

You might have a piece of corrugated plastic in your yard right now that says "For Rent," but this frosted material is as good for filtering light as it is for advertising. You can buy it in plain sheets in several solid colors from the art supply store. As for the amorphous adornment, gaze into your lava lamp for inspiration if you want to draw your own amoeba. The lamp's facade can be decorated in many other ways, as long as the added materials are translucent. Possibilities are stripes cut from colored plastics, an illustration printed on acetate, and photographic slides.

Ruler	Tubular lightbulb
Utility knife	Amoeba template
Self-healing cutting mat	Permanent marker
Sheet of white corrugated, translucent plastic	Piece of frosted orange plastic from a portfolio
Wood scrap	Scissors
Hand drill with $1/4$-inch bit	Spray adhesive
Hot glue gun and glue sticks	Four $1/4$ x 4-inch machine screws
Lamp socket	Eight $1/4$-inch washers
6-foot lamp wire with plug	Eight $1/4$-inch nuts
Screwdriver	Four $1/4$-inch acorn-shaped end caps

1. Using the ruler, utility knife, and mat, cut two 10-inch squares from the corrugated plastic. Also cut five 2-inch squares.

2. Protect your work surface with a wood scrap. Stack the two large squares so that their edges are aligned, then use the drill to make a hole near each corner.

3. Hot glue the five small squares on top of each other, then glue one side of the stack onto one of the large squares, horizontally centered and near the bottom.

LIGHTING

4. Separate the parts of the lamp socket. Pass the lamp wire through the socket's end cap, then wrap the lamp wires around the appropriate terminal screws of the socket interior (following the manufacturer's instructions) and tighten the screws. Snap the socket cover in place over the socket interior, then screw in the bulb. Glue the socket onto the top 2-inch square.

5. Enlarge the amoeba template on a copier, then use the permanent marker to trace it onto the orange plastic. Cut inside the lines with scissors. Use spray adhesive to glue the amoeba onto the remaining 10-inch square. (See figure 5.)

6. Put the screws through the holes in the lamp's back piece, their heads sticking out the backside. Put a washer on each, then a nut, and tighten the nuts. Put another nut about 1 inch down on each screw, followed by a washer. Pass the screw ends through the holes on the lamp's front piece. Put an end cap on the end of each screw, then tighten the nuts. Plug in the light and turn it on.

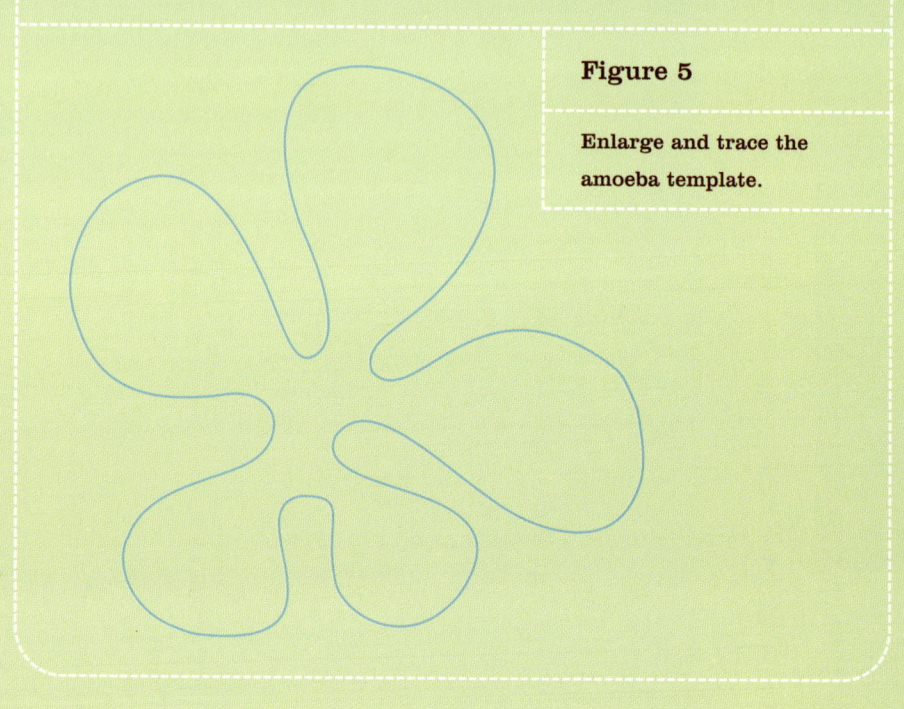

Figure 5

Enlarge and trace the amoeba template.

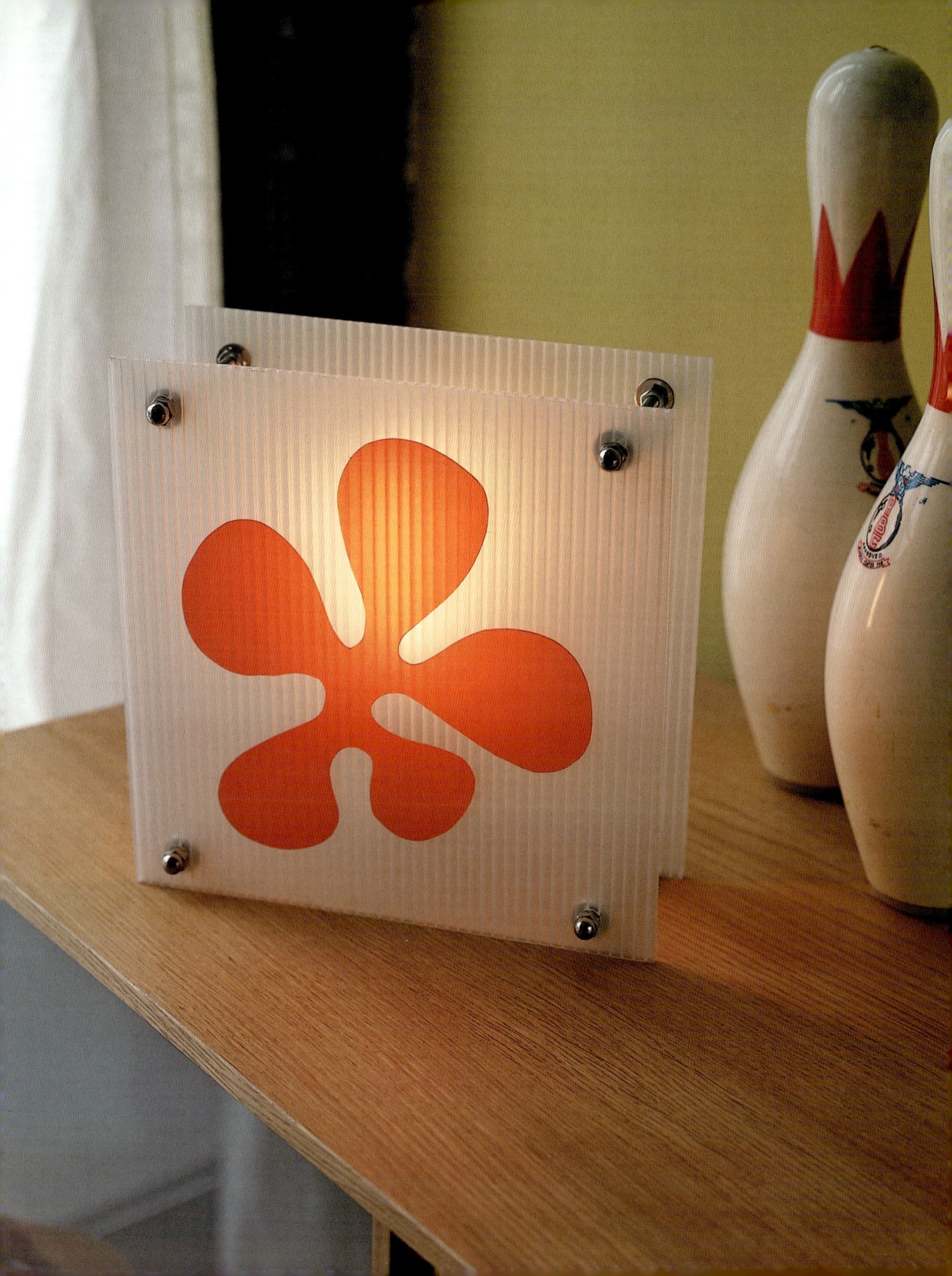

LIGHTING

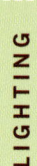

adjustable globe ceiling fixture

Put the craft staples of your youth—poster board and hobby wire—back to work in this sumptuous hanging fixture. The slats swivel around so you can adjust the light shining through, and their vents allow the bulb's heat to escape.

Twenty-one $1/8$-IP hex nuts (IP stands for "iron pipe," the standard measurement of lighting parts)
Two 3-inch $1/8$-IP threaded nipples
Lamp socket with $1/8$-IP thread
Wire cutters
Long ruler
18-gauge hobby wire
Needle-nose pliers
Utility knife
Self-healing cutting mat
Pencil
Two 22 x 28-inch white poster boards
Lamp wire in your desired length
Scissors or wire stripper
Screwdriver
60-watt lightbulb
Ceiling canopy with installation hardware

---

1. Put two nuts on the end of one nipple. Put one nut and the lamp socket's end cap on the end of the other nipple.

2. Cut a 15-inch length of hobby wire. Wrap 2 inches of each end around the nipples—between the two nuts of one nipple and between the nut and socket cap of the other. Tighten the wrapped wire with the pliers if needed, and tighten the nuts around it. Curve the wire to make room for the bulb, making sure that the nipples point toward each other. The space between the nipples should now be about 8 inches. (See figure 6.)

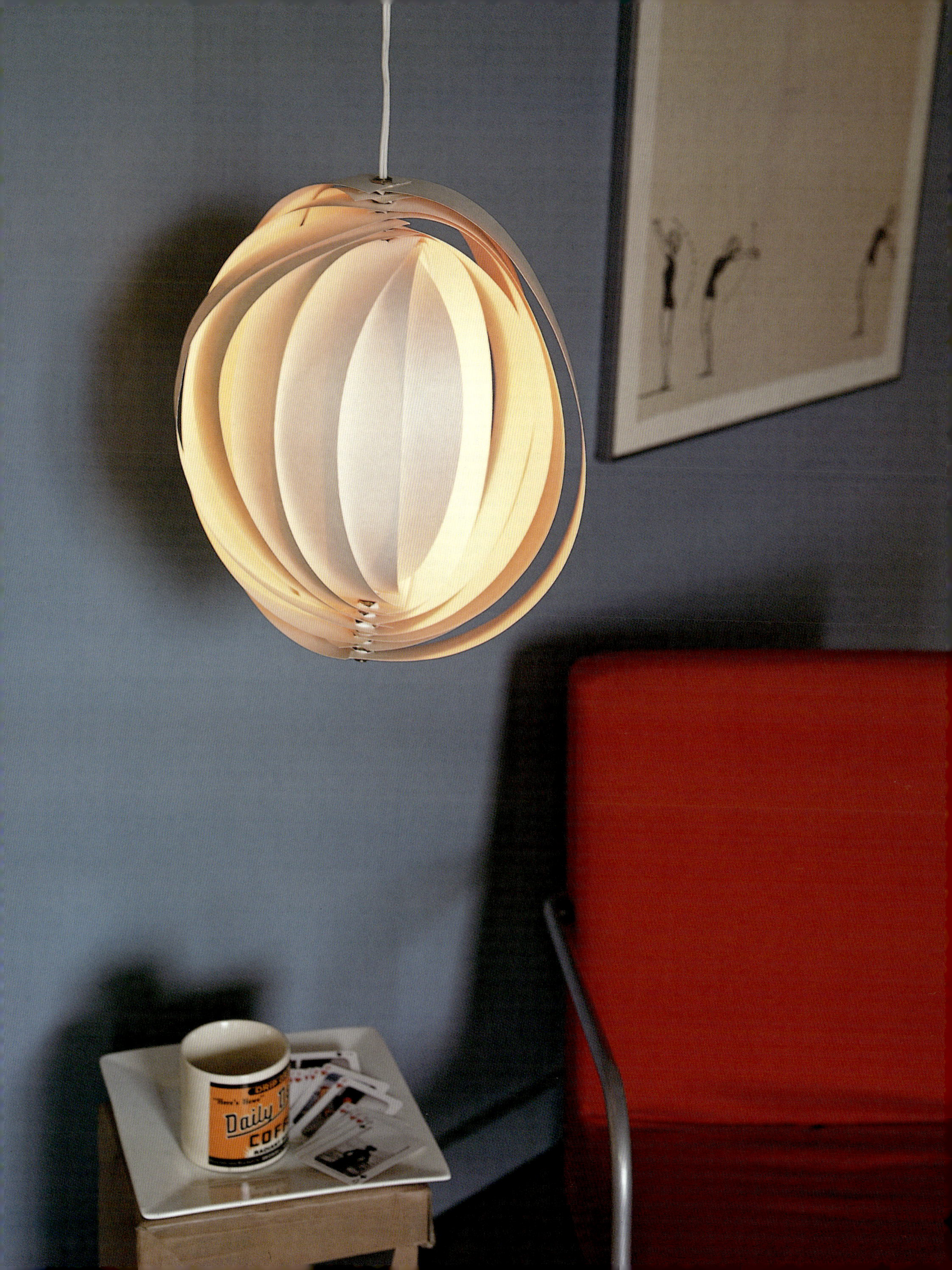
Daily

Figure 6

Nipple
Nut
Socket end cap
8"
Hobby wire
Nuts
Nipple

3. Use the utility knife and mat to cut pairs of 2-inch-wide strips of poster board to these lengths: 14, 15, 16, 17, 18, 19, 20, 21, and 22 inches. Keep the pairs in order, from shortest to longest. Cut a small X near the end of each strip and fold back the flaps to create a slot for the nipple to slide through.

4. Slide the pair of shortest strips over both nipples, keeping the strips on opposite sides. Add a nut to each nipple afterward to hold the strips in place. The two bowed strips now form a circle. Proceeding in order, starting with the next shortest pair, add the rest of the strips, anchoring each pair with nuts.

5. Use scissors or a wire stripper to cut away 1 inch of insulation from the neutral and hot wires on each end of the lamp wire. Thread one end of the wire down through the top nipple and out the socket cap. Wrap the exposed wires around the appropriate terminal screws of the socket interior: the ribbed wire is neutral and goes to the silver screw, and the smooth wire is hot and goes to the brass screw. If your socket or wires differ, follow the manufacturer's instructions for assembly. Tighten the screws, then put the socket cover over the interior and snap it in place inside the socket cap. Screw in the bulb. Slide the ceiling canopy over the exposed end of the wire.

LIGHTING

6. Turn off the power supply in the area where you will hang the fixture. The ceiling box should contain a neutral and a hot wire, probably capped with plastic nuts. (Usually, the neutral wire is black and the hot wire is white. Ask an electrician if you have doubts.) Remove the plastic nuts, twist your fixture's wires around the appropriate ceiling wires, and restore the nuts.

7. Slide the canopy up through the threaded posts in the ceiling box, pushing all the wires inside. (If your box doesn't have posts, use the mounting bracket that came with the canopy.) Screw the canopy's nuts onto the posts to fasten it to the ceiling. Restore the power supply and test your fixture. Arrange the poster strips as you like.

Have your wits about when you wire this fixture to a ceiling box. Electricity is super straightforward, but you must remember to disconnect the power supply when you handle the wires. Hire an electrician if you're uncomfortable, or buy a long length of lamp wire and a plug and turn the globe into a lantern that hooks up with a wall socket.

PRECAST CAP
STONE VENEER (CENTURION)
CERTAINTEED 'GRANDMANOR' SHINGLE IN GEORGIAN BRICK COLOR

LIGHTING

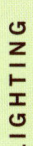

blueprint sconce

Give a second purpose to a blueprint headed for the garbage bin—architecture firms throw them away every day. Call one up, explain that you're low on mood lighting, and rescue a graphic beauty. Or someone you know may have a set left over from a building project. The soft glow of wall-mounted touch lights behind the shade is subtle; affix a bulb to wiring for a sconce, if your wall is so equipped, to achieve a bolder shine.

Utility knife
Self-healing cutting mat
Thick template plastic at least 10 x 18 inches
Long ruler
Blueprint
Pencil
Craft knife
Double-sided tape
Batteries
2 battery-operated, wall-mountable touch lights (mine have a 5½-inch diameter)
Level
2 small nails
Hammer
Metal snips
24-gauge perforated hanger iron with alternating holes for bolts and nails (found in the plumbing section of hardware stores)
4 self-drilling drywall anchors with screws, or other screws appropriate for your wall type
Screwdriver
Needle-nose pliers
Awl
2 no. 8 screws, ¼-inch long
2 no. 8 cap nuts

1. Use the utility knife and mat to cut the template plastic to 10 x 18 inches. Lay the plastic on the blueprint and determine which area you want to use. Mark around the four corners with the pencil. Slide the cutting mat under the blueprint and cut out the rectangle with the craft knife, using the edges of the plastic as your guide.

LIGHTING

2. Put double-sided tape along each edge of the plastic. Line up the blueprint cutout and slowly and carefully press it down onto the plastic. Set the sconce aside.

3. Put batteries in the two lights, set them next to each other, and measure the distance between the hanger holes on the back. Make level marks on your wall for the two nail holes, then hammer in the nails and hang the lights.

4. Use the metal snips to cut two strips of hanger iron, each with three small holes and three large holes. Hold one strip horizontally against the wall next to one light, centering the strip vertically. Make pencil marks through the two large holes closest to the light. Repeat with the other metal strip on the other side.

5. If you're mounting the sconce on drywall, use the hammer and a nail to make starter holes over your pencil marks, then screw in the self-drilling anchors. Line up the large holes of the metal strip with the anchors and drive in the screws. With the needle-nose pliers, grasp each strip beyond the screws and bend the metal toward the lights. Hold your sconce against the bent strips to test the curve created by the angled strips, and adjust the strips with the pliers as needed. (See figure 7.)

6. Lightly mark the center of each 10-inch edge of the sconce. Turn on the lights and hold up the sconce with the marks lined up with the metal strips. On each side mark a dot on the blueprint where light is shining through the small hole at the end of the strip. Use the awl to carefully punch holes here.

7. From the inside, put the no. 8 screws through the small holes in the strips. Put the holes in the sconce over the screws, then screw on the cap nuts. The sconce will want to tip forward, so have a friend hold it upright while you tighten the nuts.

LIGHTING

You don't have to use a blueprint for this sconce. Try making the fixture with a road map, illustrated instructions, or a sewing pattern.

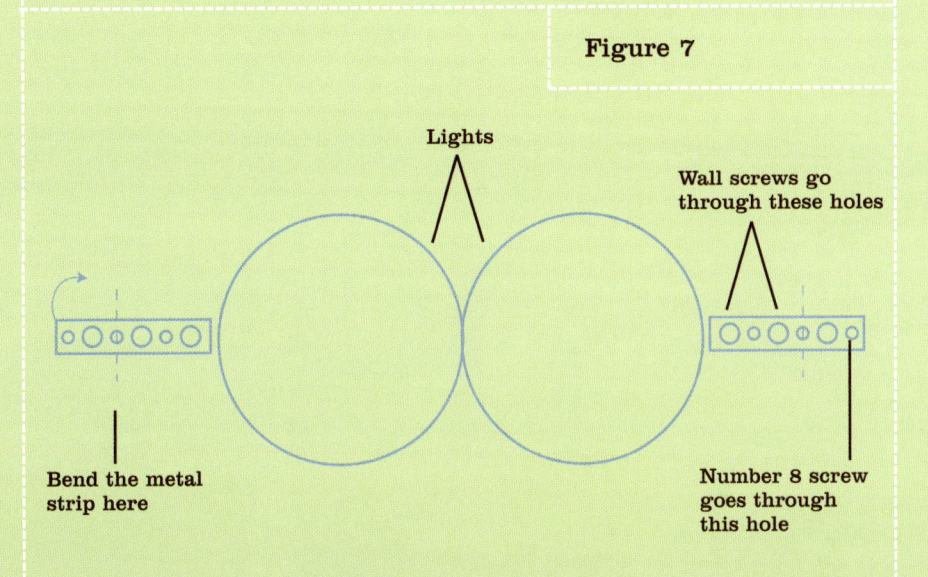

Figure 7

Lights

Wall screws go through these holes

Bend the metal strip here

Number 8 screw goes through this hole

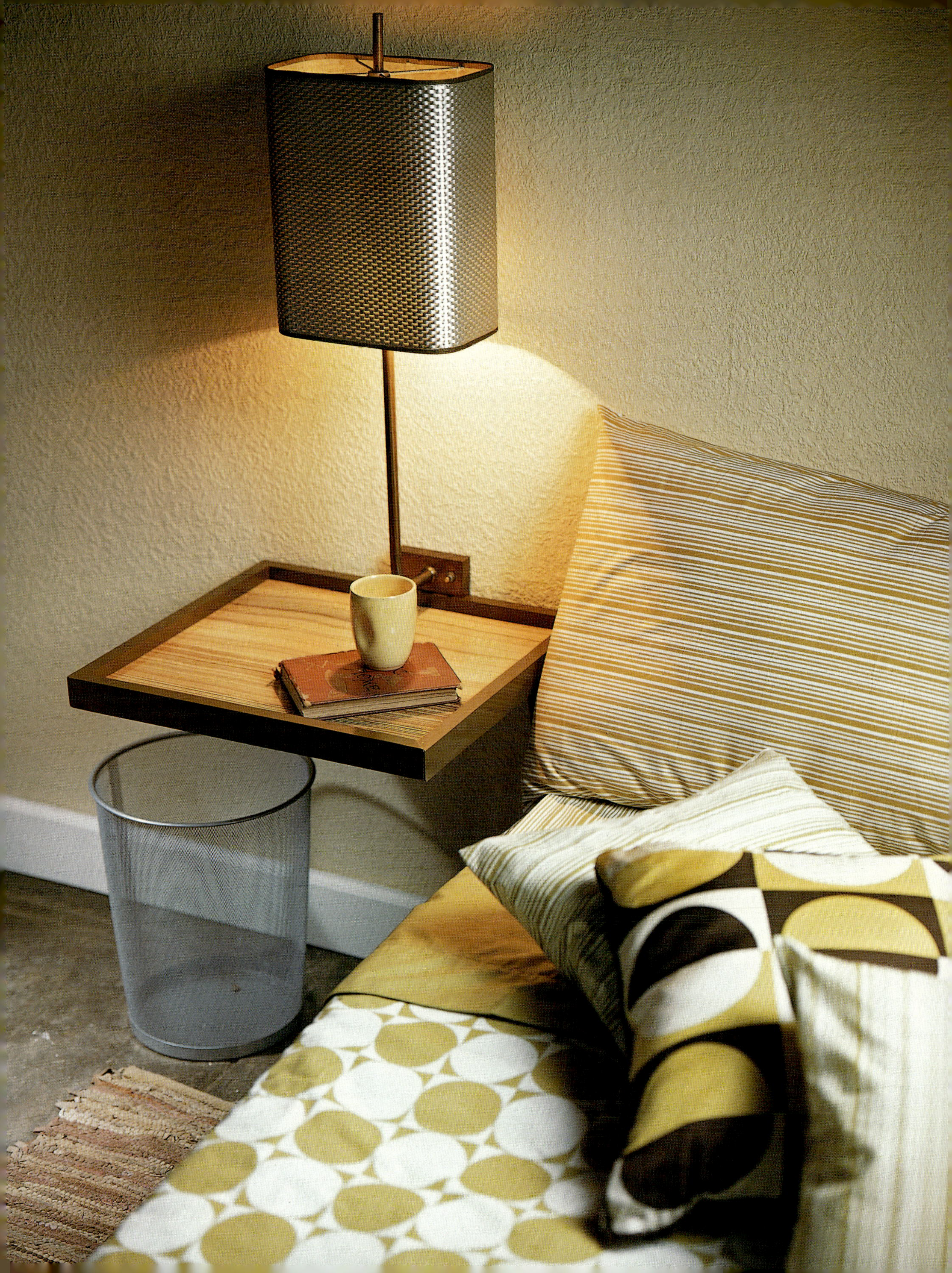

FURNITURE

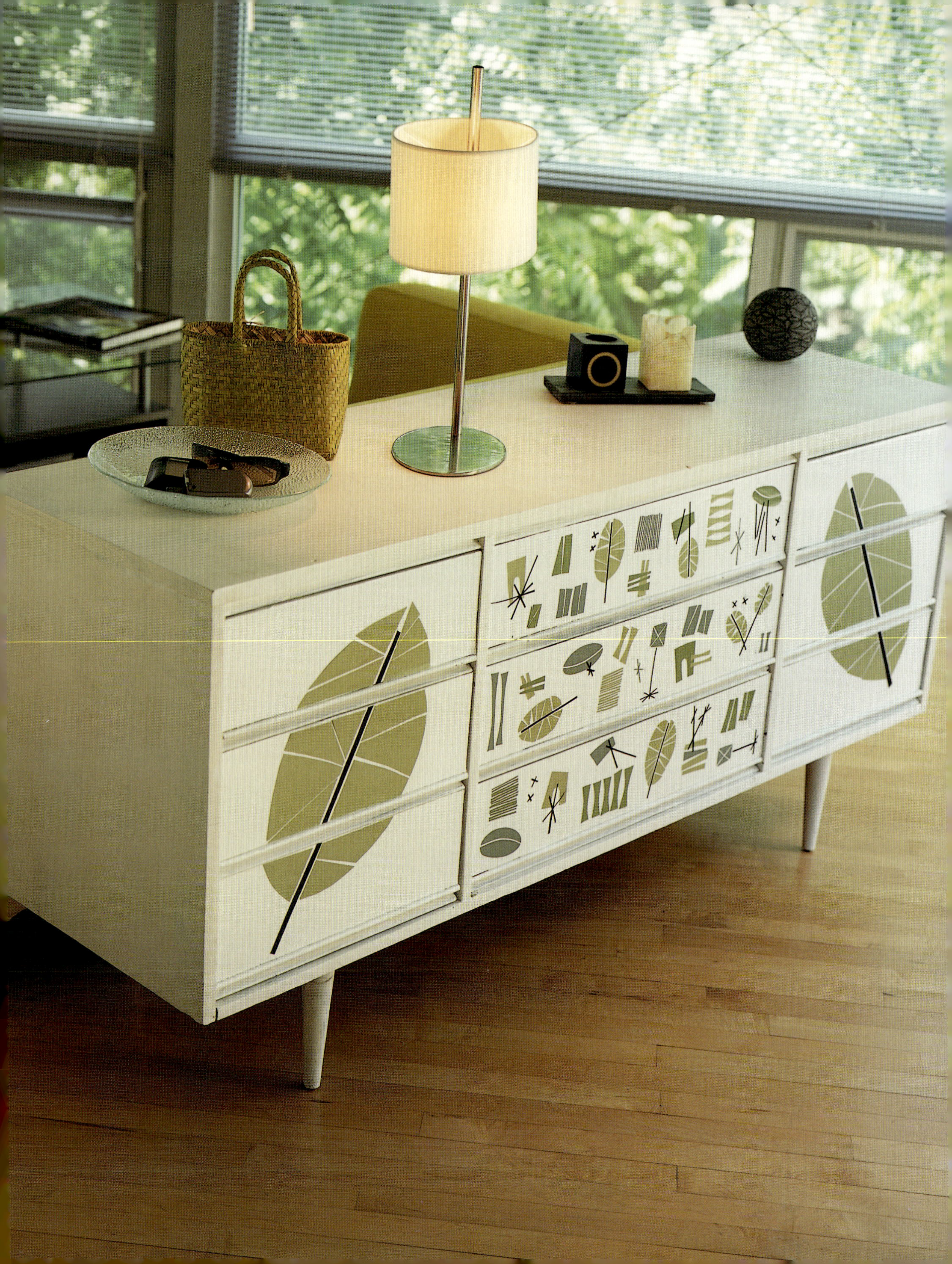

FURNITURE

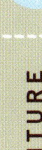

decoupaged dresser

Decoupage is a fancy French term for cutting up paper. The dancing shapes in a fifties reproduction fabric inspired me to reface my plain white dresser with lively cut-and-pasted drawing papers. See the sidebar on page 87 for fabrics that translate well into paper cutouts. If you don't want to draw your own shapes, snip apart magazines or wrapping paper instead. If you want your drawer decor to be reversible, work on adhesive-backed shelf liner instead of on the furniture itself.

Screwdriver
White adhesive-backed shelf liner (optional)
Scissors
Plastic card (a credit card works fine)
Craft knife
Inspiration fabric
Pencil

Drawing papers in the colors of your choice
Large bowl
Tape
Matte decoupage medium
Disposable bowl
Towel
Large foam paintbrush

1. Remove any drawer pulls. If you are planning to cover your drawer fronts with the shelf liner, cut pieces of liner a little larger than you need, peel off the backing, and smooth it on. Remove bubbles with the plastic card. Use the craft knife to cut off the excess liner along the drawer edges.

2. Draw the outlines of your shapes on the colored papers and cut them out. Gather the cutouts in a large bowl.

3. To make a shape that "jumps drawers," such as my leaves, tape a large piece of drawing paper over the drawers you want to cover. Sketch the shape, then use your fingernail to make creases where the paper meets the top or bottom of each drawer. Cut out the shape and cut along each crease.

4. Pour some decoupage medium into the disposable bowl. Make some interior cuts in your first shape, keeping the pieces in order on your work surface. Dip the backside of each section in the medium and place it on the dresser. Use the towel to blot off any excess glue and to maneuver the shape into position. Add more sections, leaving space between them. Repeat, one shape at a time, until the design is complete.

5. When the glue is dry, use the foam paintbrush to paint the entire front surface of the drawers with more decoupage medium. This will seal the paper's edges. Let this coat dry, then add another. When the glue is dry, replace any drawer pulls.

Decoupage medium looks milky and streaky when wet, but don't freak out. It dries perfectly clear.

FABRICS THAT REWIND THE FIFTIES

These reproduction fabrics hark back to the most dynamic period in American textile design. Not only do the characteristic shapes—some representative, some amorphous—seem to dance and play, but they also tell us what occupied the minds of their mid-twentieth-century creators. Space exploration (UFOs, satellites), nuclear technology (atomic swirls), modern art (Calder-like abstractions), travel to Hawaii (tiki masks, drums), and the myth of domestic bliss (home furnishings, cocktail glasses) all found their way onto families' sofas and curtains.

Salute this unique era of fabric design by purchasing a yard and translating its shapes into paper cutouts, then decoupaging a piece of furniture. You can painstakingly reproduce each shape by using tracing paper to transfer the pattern from the fabric to the paper, or you can just wing it with scissors like I did.

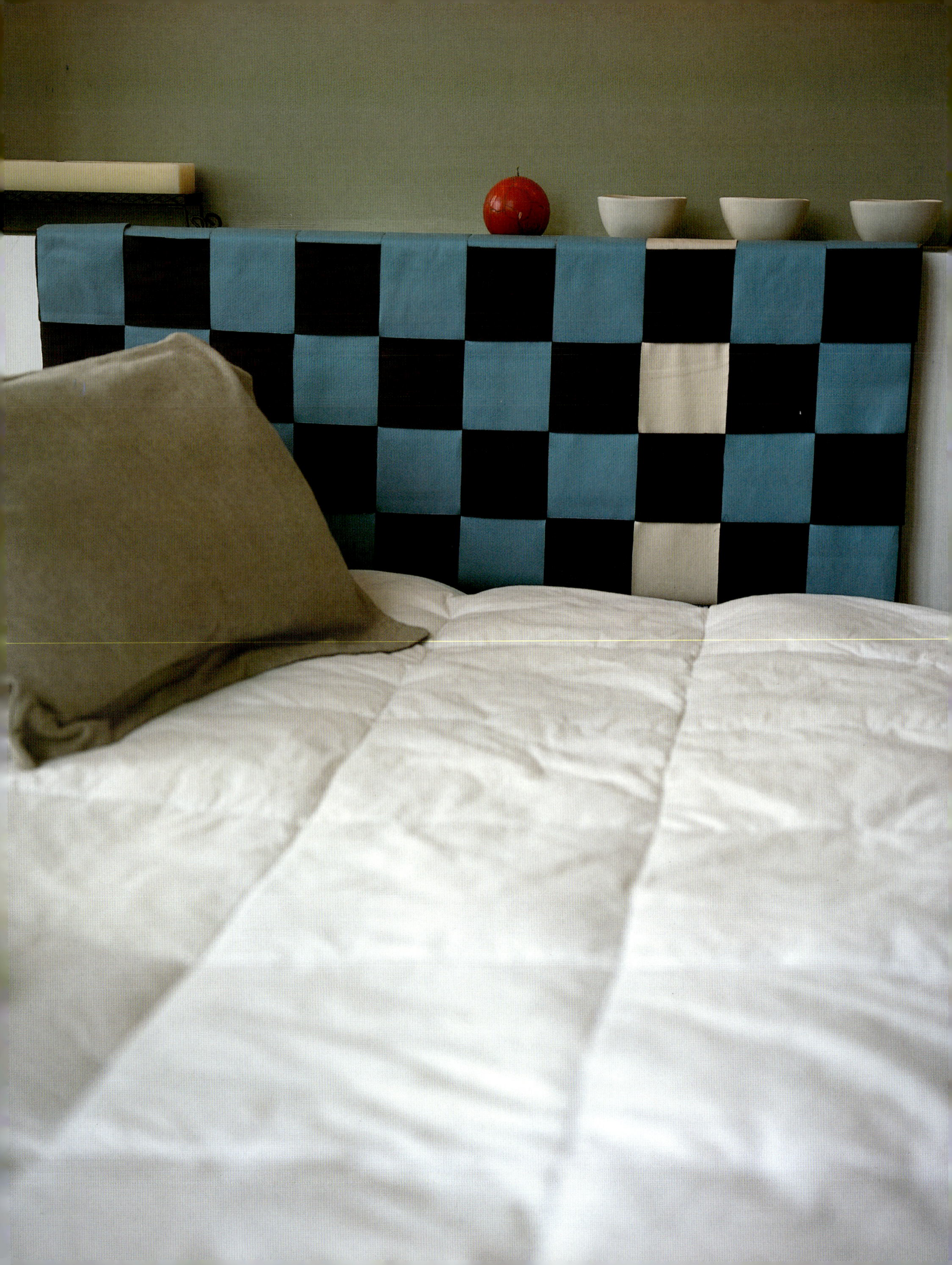

FURNITURE

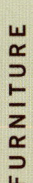

woven vinyl headboard

Many of us are plagued by rickety futons from our college days or even a mattress sitting right on the floor. You can elevate your makeshift crashing quarters to a proper bedroom with this easy-to-construct head cushion. If you are discriminating when you select your vinyl, you can fool your friends into thinking you splurged on leather. The measurements and directions are for a full-size bed; adapt them as needed for different sizes.

Long ruler or tape measure and straightedge
2-inch-thick upholstery foam, a cake at least 20 x 50 inches
Marker
Serrated knife
2 yards brown vinyl
1 yard turquoise vinyl
$1/4$ yard cream vinyl
Scissors
Straight pins
3 wreath hooks
Tape
3 nails
Hammer

1. Measure a 20 x 50-inch rectangle on the foam and draw the boundaries with the marker. Cut along the lines with the serrated knife.

2. Lay out the fabrics wrong side up and measure and mark 5-inch-wide strips. The brown strips, which run side to side, should be 60 inches long; you need 4. The turquoise and cream strips, which run up and down, should be 30 inches long; you need 9 turquoise and 1 cream. Use the side edge of your fabric as a guide for drawing parallel lines with the marker and ruler. Cut out the strips.

3. Place the turquoise strips and the one cream strip side by side on the foam. Arrange them so that the ends have an equal amount of excess and the end strips are even with the side edges of the foam. Along one side, wrap the

FURNITURE

ends to the back and pin them in place (two pins per strip), with the pins nearly parallel with the foam so that they won't poke toward the front.

4. Add the brown strips, one at a time from the unpinned end, weaving them over and under the turquoise strips. Make sure the pattern is even everywhere and no foam is showing, then pin all loose ends at the back.

5. Insert the wreath hooks in the top two corners and at the middle of the back of the foam. Ball up three pieces of tape, sticky side out, and stick a ball on top of each hook. Place the headboard against the wall at the desired height and press it just enough to transfer the tape balls to the wall. Insert nails where the tape indicates, then hang the headboard.

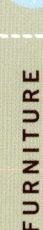

pizza pan pedestal

FURNITURE

Come on, when's the last time you made a homemade pie anyway? Put your pizza pan to a more artistic use by cooking up a graphic, gravity-defying table. Despite the skinny stem and petite base, the table is sturdy enough for light duty. Cocktails, candles, or hors d'oeuvres are the right fit. For a more robust pedestal, use a larger, heavier lamp weight.

Hacksaw
$1/8$-IP threaded rod at least 20 inches long (IP stands for "iron pipe," the standard measurement of lighting parts)
Rough-grit sandpaper
Three $1/8$-IP hex nuts
Two $1/8$-IP washers
Iron lamp weight, at least 7 pounds, with $1/8$-IP center hole
Pliers
Newspaper
Silver spray paint
Dinner plate
Template plastic
Permanent marker
Scissors
Coaster or similar size round object
Craft knife
Repositionable spray adhesive
Sturdy pizza pan with a smooth backside (mine has a 15-inch diameter)
Red spray paint
Cotton swabs
Nail polish remover
Disposable plates
Acrylic spray sealer
Plastic gloves
Two-part epoxy for metal
Craft stick
$1 1/8$-inch washer with $5/16$-inch hole
Tape measure

1. Use the hacksaw to cut down the threaded rod to 20 inches. Rub the cut end on the sandpaper to smooth it out.

2. Put a hex nut, then an $1/8$-IP washer on one end of the rod and screw it into the top of the weight until about 1 inch protrudes below. Add the other $1/8$-IP

FURNITURE

washer, then a second nut to the protruding end. Tighten the nuts with the pliers.

3. Spray the weight and rod silver.

4. Place the dinner plate on the template plastic and trace around it with the marker. Cut out the circle with scissors. Place the coaster near one edge of the plastic circle and trace it. Use the craft knife to make the initial cut inside the small circle, then cut it out with scissors. The large circle with the hole becomes your design template.

5. On your protected work surface, spray repositionable adhesive on one side of the template, then place it off center on the backside of the pizza pan. Smooth down the edges. Spray the exposed pan with the red paint, then carefully peel off the template while the paint is still wet.

6. Use cotton swabs dipped in nail polish remover to clean up your painted lines. If you need to add paint in areas, spray more red paint onto a disposable plate, then use cotton swabs as paintbrushes.

7. When the pan is dry, spray on two coats of acrylic sealer.

8. Wear the plastic gloves when you work with the two-part epoxy. Put small, equal amounts on a disposable plate and stir them together with the craft stick. Glue together the remaining hex nut and the $1^{1}/_{8}$-inch washer, lining up their center holes. Let the glue cure for the manufacturer's recommended time.

9. Use the tape measure and marker to locate the center point of the pan on its unpainted side. Mix more epoxy, then glue the washer of the washer-nut combo in the center. Let the glue cure, then screw the pan onto the threaded rod.

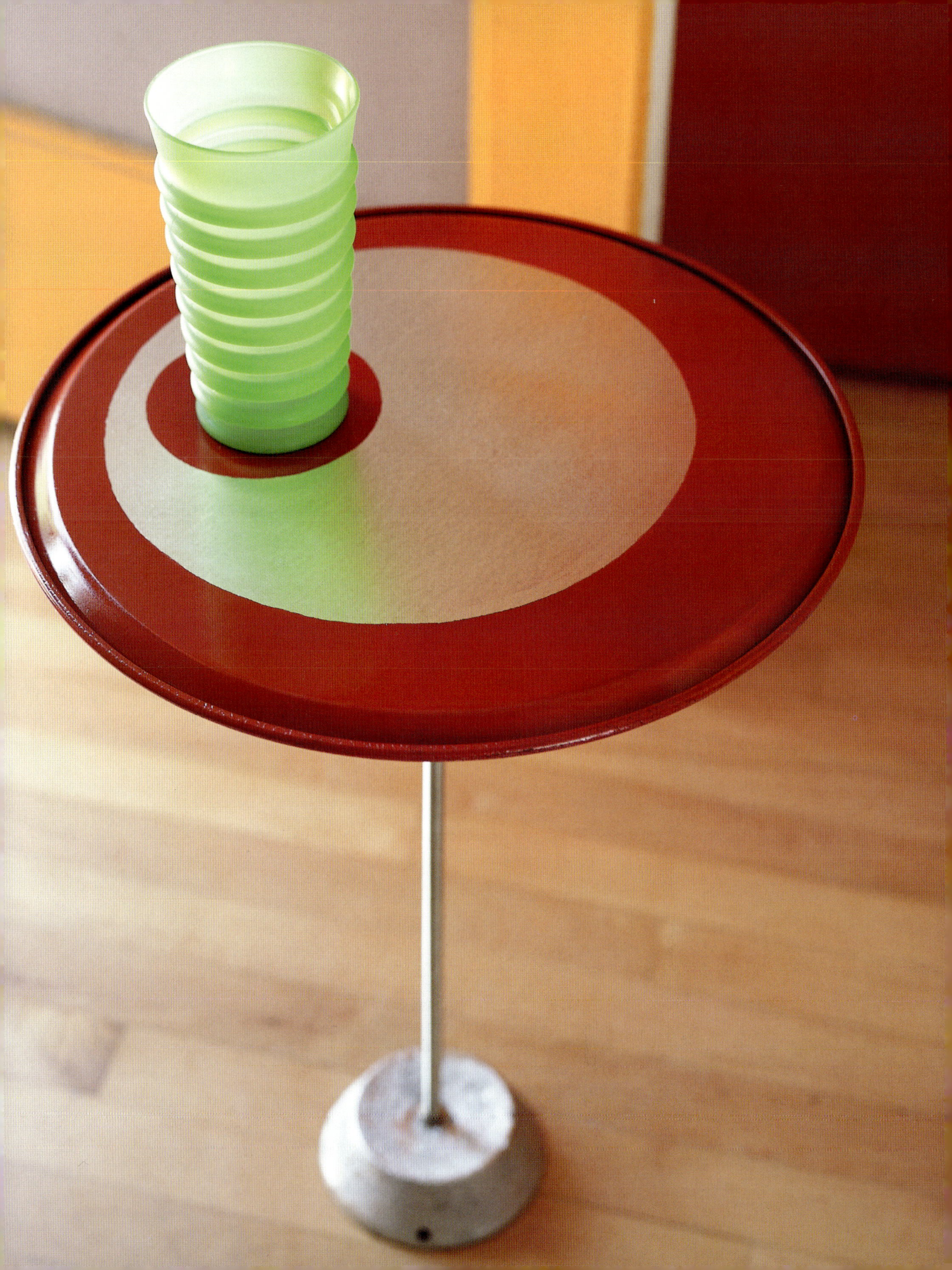

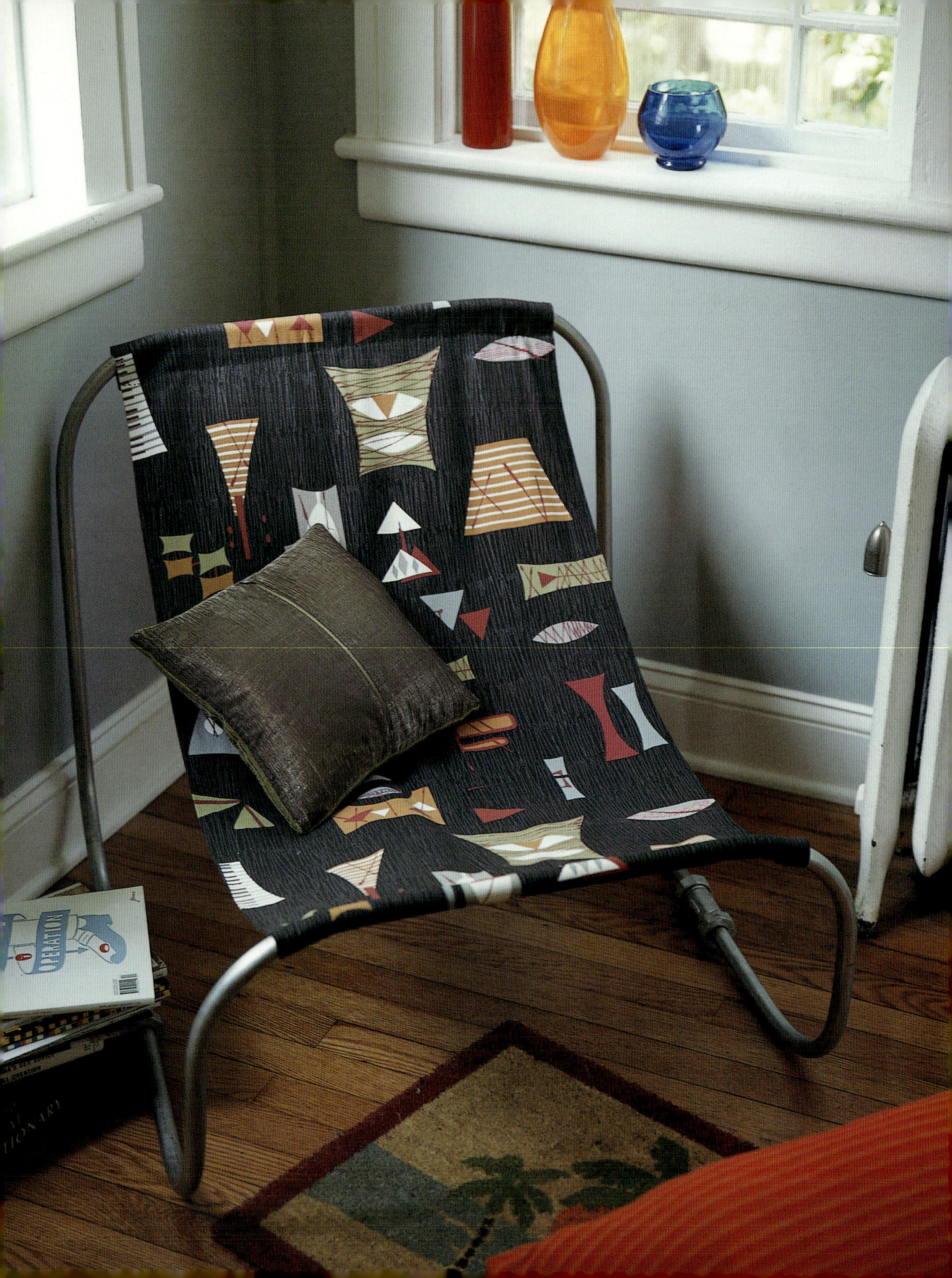
OPERATION

FURNITURE

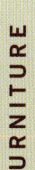

low sling chair

Many didn't think it could be done, but I was determined to make a real piece of furniture out of electrical conduit, the pipes that hide wires inside your walls. The faithless said that my chair would bow or break, and it did both—at first. My debut seat promptly but gently delivered me to the floor. The version I present now will support your bum securely as long as you use the better-quality (but still inexpensive) rigid conduit, not the wimpy sort labeled EMT.

1½ yards upholstery-weight fabric
Pencil
L-shaped ruler
Scissors
Straight pins
Iron and ironing board
Iron-on seam tape
Sewing needle
Upholstery-weight thread in coordinating color

Two 10-foot lengths ½-inch rigid conduit (not EMT)
Tape measure
Crayon
Pipe bender
Pipe cutter
Two ½-inch compression couplings for unthreaded pipe

1. On the wrong side of the fabric, use the pencil and L-shaped ruler to mark a 43 x 23-inch rectangle. Cut it out.

2. Pin a 1-inch hem along the two long edges. Iron the hems, remove the pins, and secure the hems with the seam tape. Pin a 3½-inch hem along the two short edges, and stitch them with the needle and thread. Stitch two rows per hem for extra strength, and lock the stitches by reversing at the beginning and end of each row.

3. You'll make 90-degree bends in the two conduits based on the diagram. Use the tape measure and crayon to mark your first bend on the conduit

FURNITURE

(15 inches from one end). See your pipe bender's instructions for the correct placement of the tool in relation to your mark. Position the bender, stand on the conduit on the side you aren't bending (you may need a helper to stand on it as well), and rock the tool toward you until the bend measures 90 degrees. Verify the angle with the L-shaped ruler. Measure and mark your next bend (either 15 inches or 25 inches, depending on whether you're making the chair back or the front), rotate the conduit 90 degrees, and make the bend. (See figure 8.)

4. After you have made all the bends in both pieces of conduit, remove the excess pipe with the pipe cutter. Check that the two sides of the chair fit together.

5. Slide the fabric seat onto the two sides of the chair. Connect the chair halves with the compression couplings. Tighten them as much as you can.

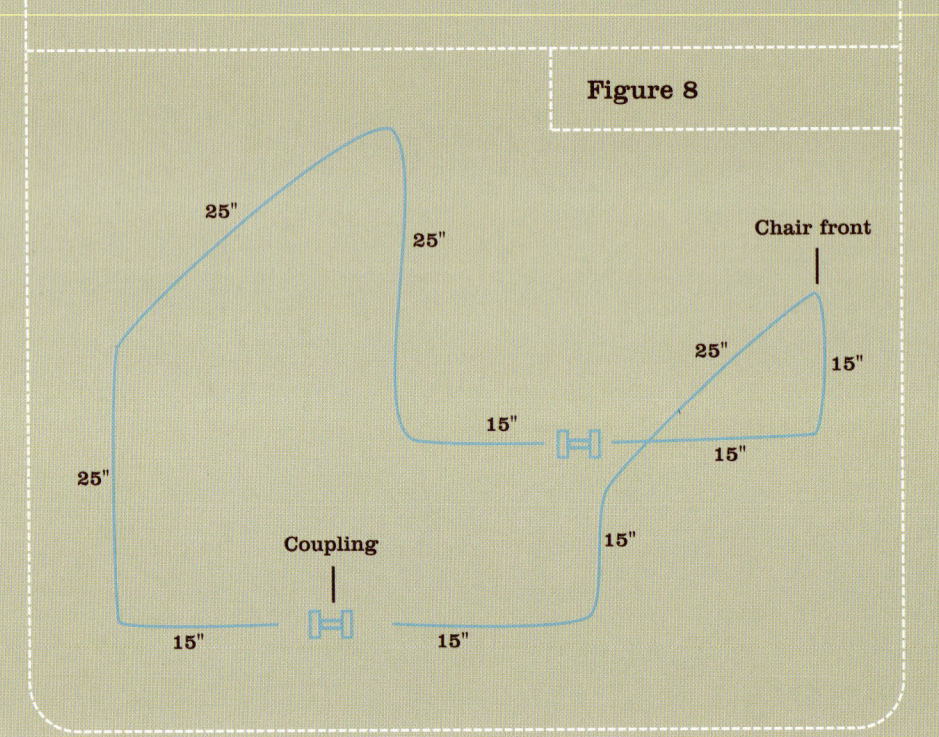

Figure 8

FURNITURE

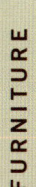

rolling two-tier coffee table

Sometimes contrast is what makes a creation work—clunky plumbing parts and sleek shelf boards harmonize well in this simple table. The casters let it roll where you need it, and the lower level is great for displaying your prized periodicals and a certain fantastic decorating book.

Eight 1-inch galvanized flanges
2 MDF shelf boards laminated with white melamine, $3/4$ inch thick, 16 inches wide, and 48 inches long
Ruler
Pencil
Hammer and nail
Screwdriver
Forty-eight $1/2$-inch wood screws with large heads
Four 1 x 12-inch galvanized pipe nipples
4 small metal casters
White latex paint, if needed
Paintbrush

1. Place a flange on a shelf board $2 1/2$ inches in from the short edge and $1 1/2$ inches in from the long edge. Mark a dot on the shelf through each of the flange's four holes. Repeat in the other three corners. Make starter holes on these marks with the hammer and nail.

2. Screw down a flange in each corner, then attach a pipe nipple to each flange. Top off each nipple with the remaining flanges.

3. Put the other shelf board on top of the flanges so that it lines up with the lower board. Mark a dot through each flange hole, make starter holes, then attach the flanges to the board with screws.

FURNITURE

4. Select the less attractive side of the table to be the bottom. Line up a caster with each corner, mark a dot through each hole, make starter holes, and attach the casters with screws.

5. Paint any raw edges of the shelf boards white.

If your shelf boards have raw edges, you can iron on $3/4$-inch melamine tape as an alternative to painting them if you like.

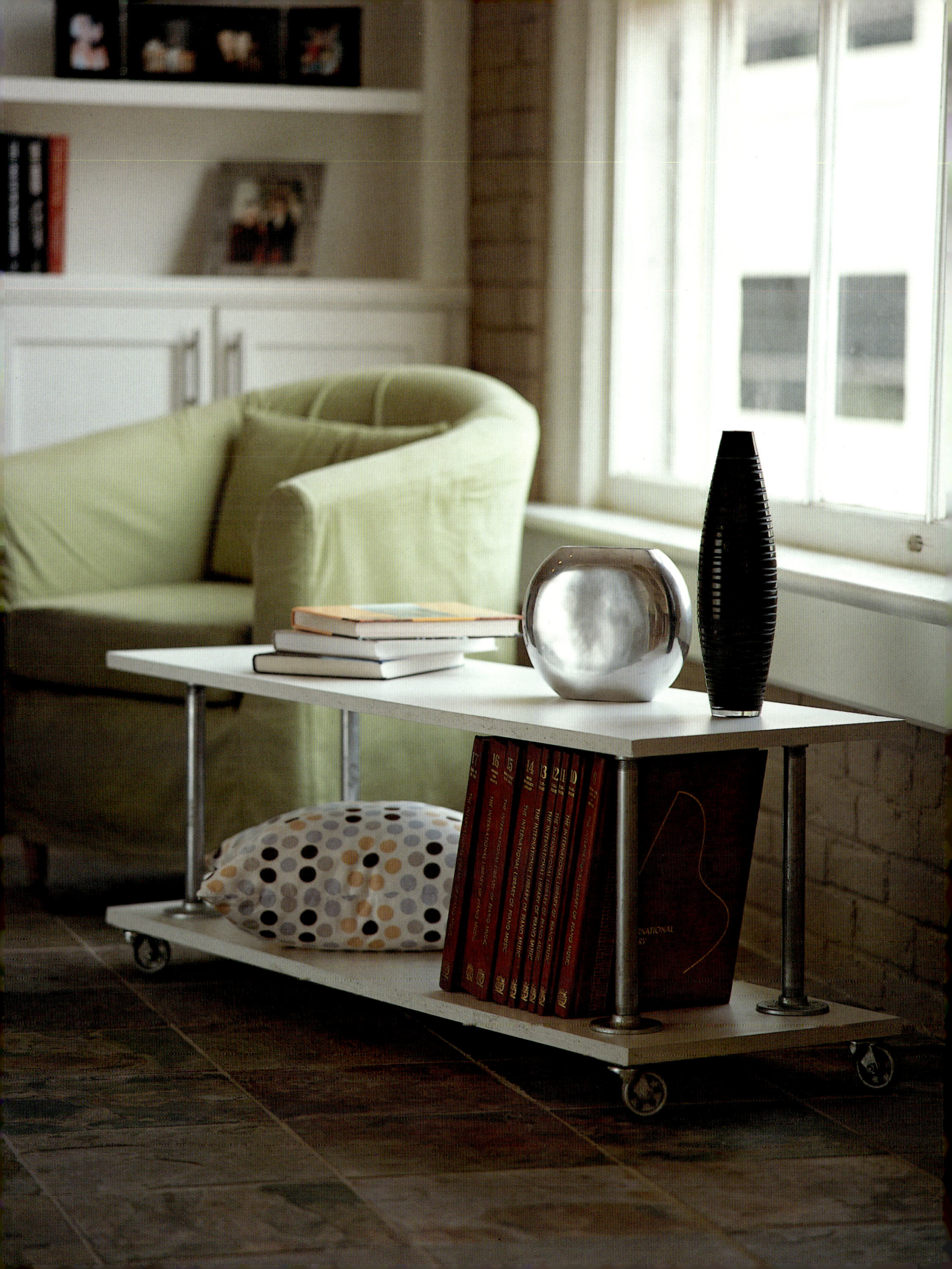

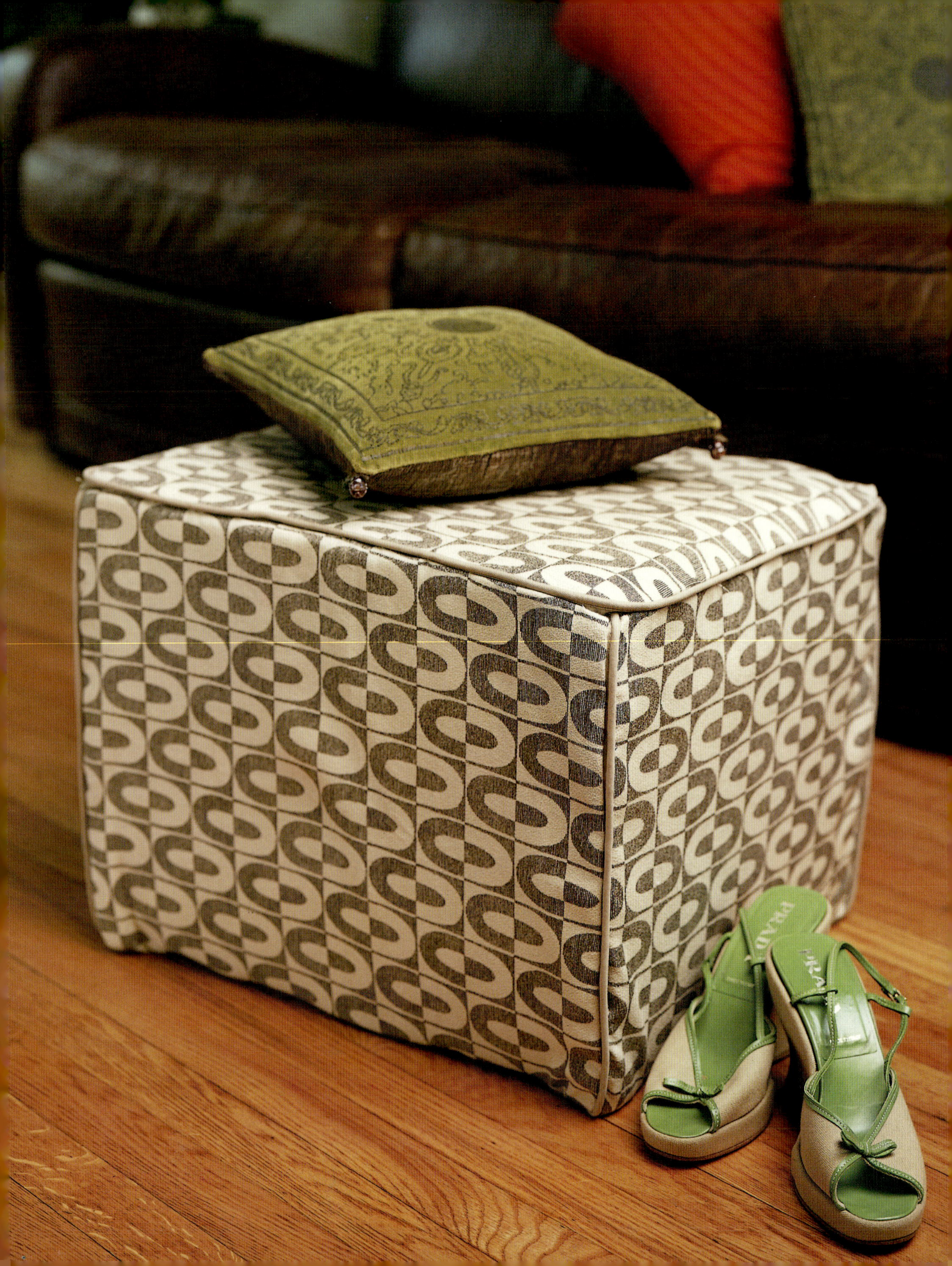

slipcovered crate ottoman

Have you seen the outrageous price tags on ottomans? They cost nearly as much as the chairs they accompany. This homemade version has humble bones, but you can splurge on the fabric to make the outcome look high end. I recommend staples to assemble the fabric and trim for all you nonsewers out there, but machine stitches make this project more durable.

FURNITURE

At least 8 square feet of 1-inch-thick foam
Long ruler
Marker
Scissors
Hot glue gun and glue sticks
14 x 17 x 10½-inch plastic crate
Cake of 4-inch-thick foam at least 16 x 19 inches
Long serrated knife
1½ yards upholstery-weight fabric
Pencil
4 yards coordinating piping
Straight pins
Office-type stapler and staples

1. Draw the following dimensions on the 1-inch foam using the ruler and marker: two rectangles at 10½ x 16 inches and two at 10½ x 17. Cut out the foam with scissors.

2. Hot glue the 17-inch-long foam pieces to the crate sides of that length. Glue the 16-inch-long pieces to the 14-inch-long sides (they will overlap the foam on the adjacent side). If your crate has protrusions for stacking, apply the glue to these.

3. Draw a 16 x 19-inch rectangle on the 4-inch foam and cut it out with the serrated knife. Hot glue the foam to the crate bottom (which henceforth will be called the top, since it's the ottoman's seat).

4. On the wrong side of the fabric, use the pencil to mark the dimensions of the slipcover. For the ottoman's sides, two panels at 17 1/2 x 17 inches and two at 17 1/2 x 20 inches. For the top, 17 x 20 inches. Cut out the fabric panels and separate them by size.

5. Cut four 17 1/2-inch lengths of piping and set aside the remainder.

6. Join the side panels like this: Lay down a 17 1/2 x 17-inch panel, pattern side up, with the 17 1/2-inch edge near you. Lay a piece of cut piping, with its flat part facing you, 1/2 inch in from the fabric's near edge. Pin it in place. Lay down a 17 1/2 x 20-inch panel, pattern side down, with its 17 1/2-inch edge in line with the near edge of the bottom fabric and pin it in place. With the stapler in one hand, feel for the round part of the piping with your free hand and apply staples through the three layers, about 1/2 inch apart, as close as possible to the round part of the piping. Remove the pins. Continue to attach the remaining side panels by alternating the sizes and lining up the 17 1/2-inch edges. (See figure 9.)

7. Lay down the top fabric panel, pattern side up, and pin the remaining piping along all four edges, beginning and ending at the same corner. The flat part of the piping should be 1/2 inch in from the edge and facing outward. Cut off any excess piping.

8. To join the top panel to the side panels, slip the sides onto the ottoman inside out. Center the top panel over the top of the ottoman, pattern side down, and pin its edges to the side panels' edges. All around the perimeter, staple through the two fabrics and the flat part of the piping as in step 6. Remove the pins.

FURNITURE

9. Turn the slipcover right side out and put it back on the ottoman. Pull down the fabric firmly. Flip over the ottoman, turn under the loose edges, and hot glue them to the inside of the crate.

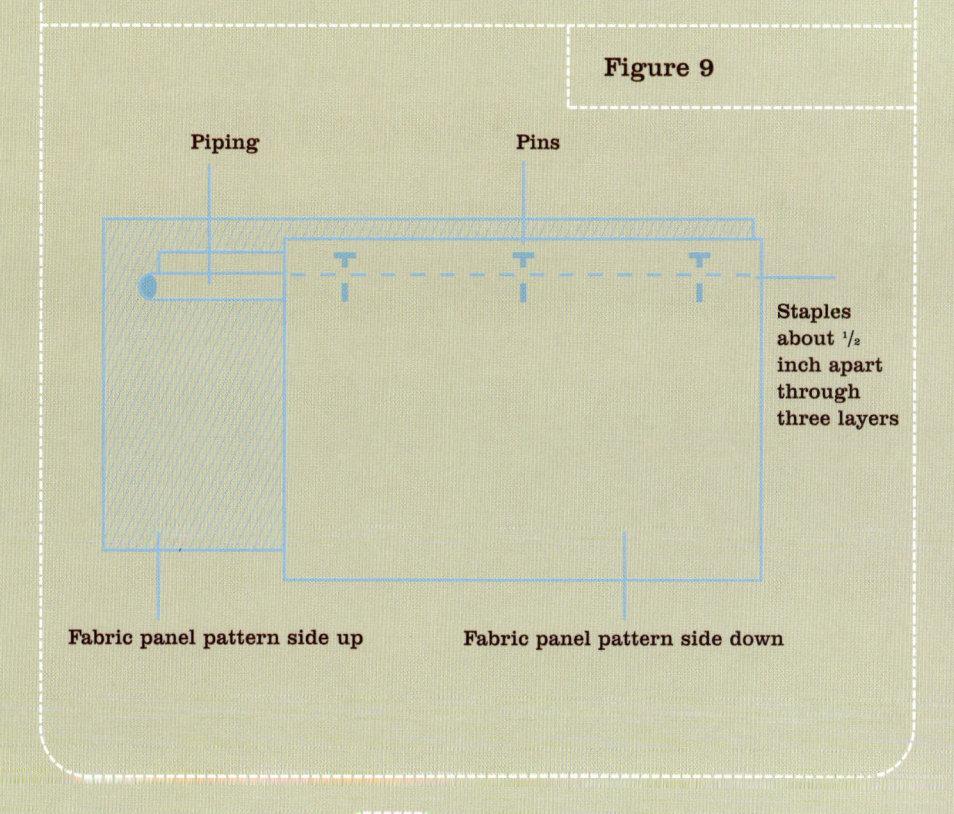

Figure 9

Piping

Pins

Staples about 1/2 inch apart through three layers

Fabric panel pattern side up

Fabric panel pattern side down

103

FURNITURE

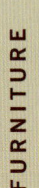

canvas folding screen

Who couldn't use a screen to hide a home office or define a dressing area? This project is my most expensive because of the sixteen heavy-duty canvas stretchers that form its frame, but the price is not too high for a sturdy piece of furniture that will divide your space stylishly for years. Convenience trumps thriftiness here: the stretchers have tongue-and-groove mitered corners that you simply bang together for perfect 90-degree angles. You can save some dough by making your skeleton from 1 x 2 lumber, glue, and corrugated fasteners if you like.

Hammer	Oval-shaped template, such as a serving platter
Eight 16-inch heavy-duty canvas stretchers	Pencil
Eight 72-inch heavy-duty canvas stretchers	Tape measure
Scissors	Towel
14 yards red canvas	Washcloth (optional)
Staple gun and staples	Spray starch
Iron and ironing board	Six 1$\frac{1}{2}$-inch hinges with screws
2 yards fusible webbing	Nail
1 yard white canvas	Screwdriver

1. Use the hammer to assemble the tongue-and-groove joints of the canvas stretchers to make four 16 x 72-inch frames.

2. Cut the entire length of red canvas into four equal quadrants. Put one panel on your work surface and set a frame on top. Wrap the excess canvas around the frame and attach it by starting with a staple in the middle of one long edge, then pulling the fabric taut and putting a staple in the opposite edge. Move a few inches from your first staple and apply another, then another on the opposite edge. Repeat on the short edges, but leave the corners for last. Make hospital folds, as with bedsheets, to hide the excess fabric at the corners and staple them. Cover the remaining three frames in this way.

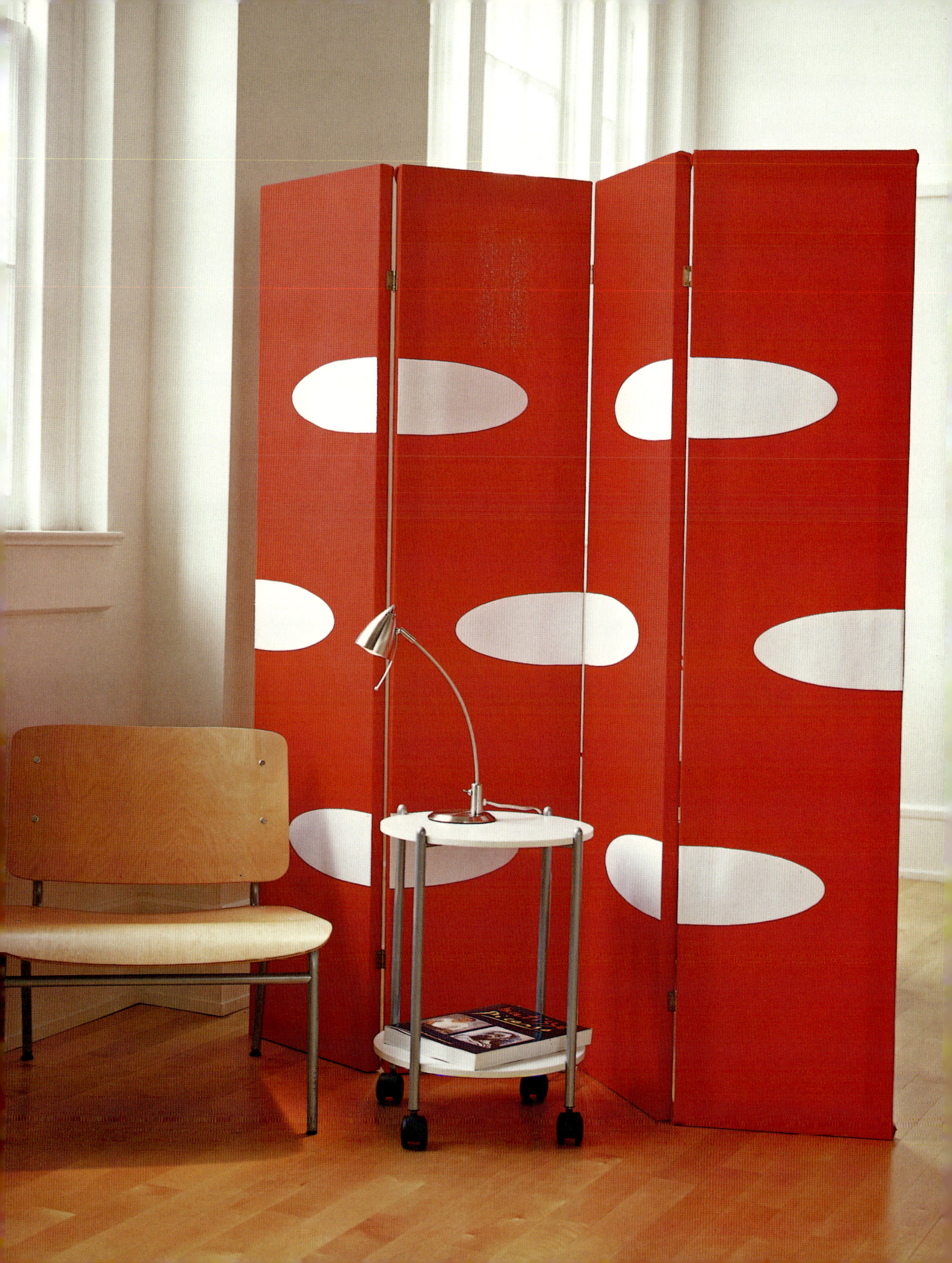

3. Set your iron temperature according to the instructions of your fusible webbing. Cover the white canvas with abutting strips of webbing. Iron the webbing gently until it adheres, smoothing out any wrinkles.

4. Put the oval platter on the backside of the webbing-backed fabric and trace around it six times. Cut out the ovals, then cut them in half across the short diameter. Lightly mark the center of each half-oval's straight edge.

5. Along one long edge of each red panel, mark a dot at 18 and 54 inches. Mark a dot at 36 inches on the opposite edge. Put a folded towel under a right-side-up panel, centered under one of the marks you just made. Remove the paper backing from a half-oval and line up its pencil mark with the one on the panel. If your webbing's instructions call for a pressing cloth, dampen the washcloth. Iron the half-oval until it is completely adhered to the red canvas. Repeat with all the half-ovals, then spray them with starch to keep their edges from fraying.

6. Lean all the completed panels against a wall in the order you will assemble them. Begin with the leftmost panel. Put a mark 6 inches from the top and 6 inches from the bottom along its right edge. Center a hinge over each mark and draw a dot through the screw holes. Make starter holes on the marks with the hammer and nail, then screw in two hinges in the direction that will allow the backs of the first and second panel to bend toward each other.

7. Line up the first and second panels, mark the attached hinges' holes onto the second panel, make starter holes, then screw in the hinges. Attach the remaining panels in this way, except that where the second and third panels are joined, attach the hinges in the direction that will allow them to fold the panels' fronts toward each other.

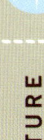

"zebrawood" bedside tables

FURNITURE

These chocolate-framed tray tables pair deliciously with a platform bed or even a mattress on the floor. The rare zebrawood they mimic, named for its high-contrast striped grain, is imported from Africa for the rich and famous. You can get the look without the cost or pomp with a glaze-and-combing technique for equally fabulous and one-of-a-kind furniture.

- Newspaper
- Beige latex paint
- Paintbrush
- 16 x 36-inch MDF shelf board (unlaminated) cut in half lengthwise at your hardware store to make two 16 x 18-inch pieces
- Miter saw and miter box
- Dark brown latex paint
- 13 feet of 1 x 2 pine
- Cardboard
- Scissors
- Faux finishing glaze
- Disposable container
- Paint stirrer
- Poster board
- Nail polish remover, if needed
- Paper towels, if needed
- Spray polyurethane
- Hand drill with bits
- Hammer
- Finish nails
- Countersink
- Wood filler
- Fine sandpaper
- Pencil
- Level
- 4 metal wall brackets with a dark wood finish and mounting hardware appropriate for your wall type
- Four $1/2$-inch wood screws (optional)

1. Cover your work surface with newspaper. Paint one side of each MDF board beige. Let it dry, then paint a second coat.

2. With the miter saw and box, stand the pine on its short edge and cut it at 45-degree angles. You need four pieces that measure 16 inches at the inner edge and four that measure 18 inches. The cuts at the end of each piece should

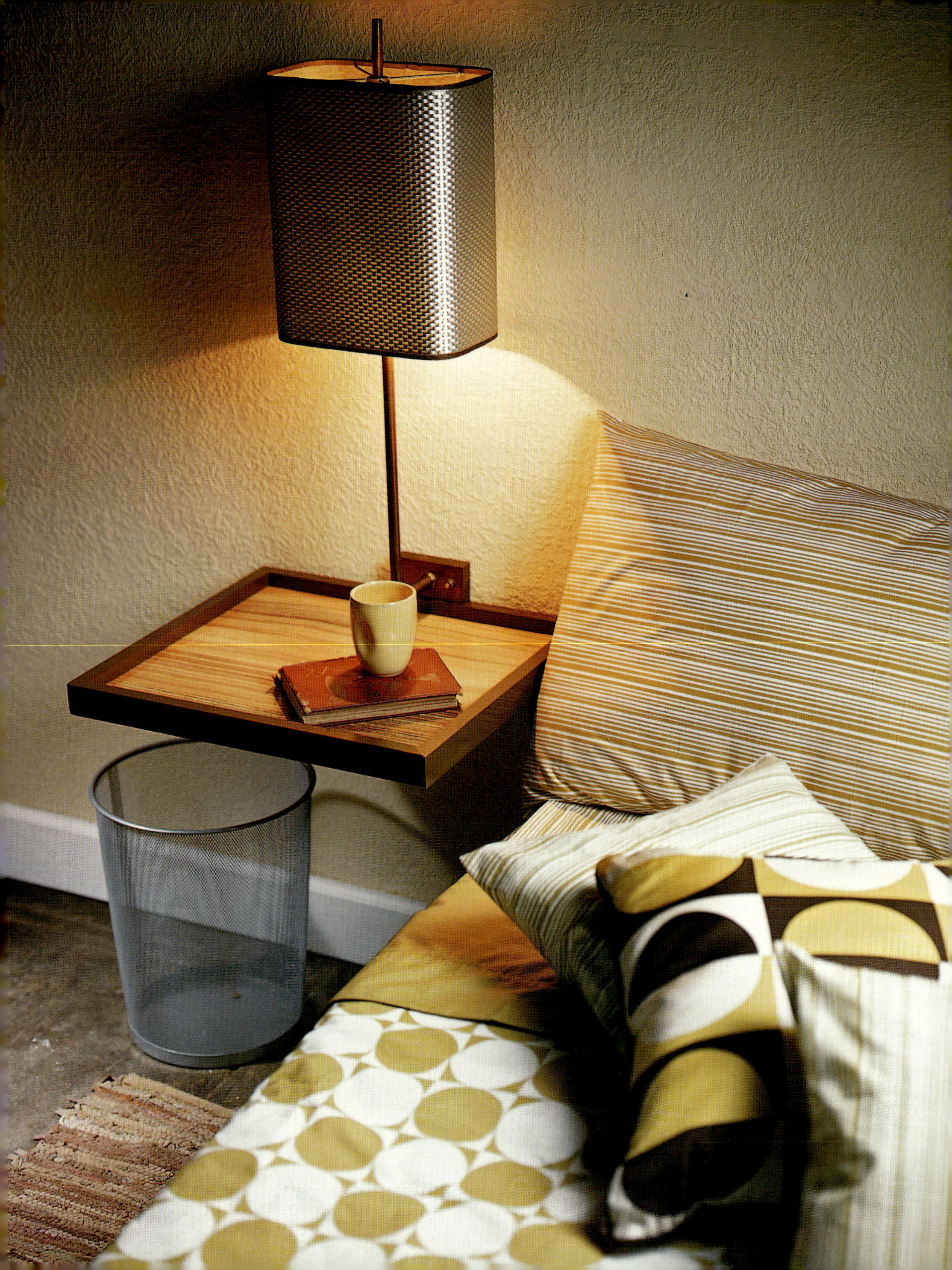

FURNITURE

angle outward. Test the cut pieces around your MDF for fit; make adjustments if necessary.

3. Paint the wood pieces brown. Let them dry, then paint a second coat.

4. Make at least 15 cardboard combs for creating the striped "grain." Cut out rectangles, varying the length between 3 and 6 inches. Along one long edge of each, cut slits about $1/16$ inch wide. Don't measure, though, just quickly cut to get random sizes. Rub the sliced edges on a rough surface such as a brick wall to fan out the slits a bit. (See figure 10.)

5. Pour one part brown paint to four parts glaze into the disposable container and mix thoroughly. Practice your combing technique. Paint an even layer of glaze mixture onto the poster board. Comb through the glaze with a piece of cardboard in one smooth motion. Quickly set aside that comb, pick up another, and comb the area next to your first pass. Do not reuse combs. Vary your pressure and hand motion to discover different effects.

6. When you feel confident, use the combing technique on the tables. Make your grain parallel with the long sides. Be sure to begin and end each pass of a comb at an edge. If you make a mistake, quickly clean off the entire surface with nail polish remover and paper towels and start over.

FURNITURE

7. Let your grain dry, then spray the tables with three coats of polyurethane to protect your design.

8. To assemble the trim around the tables, have a friend stand one on its side and hold a piece of the pine against the top edge. Predrill several nail holes, one near each end and a couple in between. Hammer in the nails and countersink the heads. Repeat on the remaining edges and for the second table.

9. Dab wood filler over the sunken nails and in any corner gaps. Let it dry, then sand it flush. Wipe off the dust and touch up the brown paint.

10. To install each table, draw a level line at the desired height on the wall and hang two brackets. Set the table on top. If you like, secure the table to the brackets with screws.

Figure 10

Cardboard comb

Cut slits about 1/16" wide.

RECYCLED DRINK MARKERS

Reuse greeting cards, calendars, and other colorful card stocks to mark your guests' glasses at your next cocktail party. Cut out two same-size chunks that are larger than you need, and glue the wrong sides together. Set a book on top while the sandwich dries, then cut out the shape you want and add a slit for the rim of the glass.

minute mod

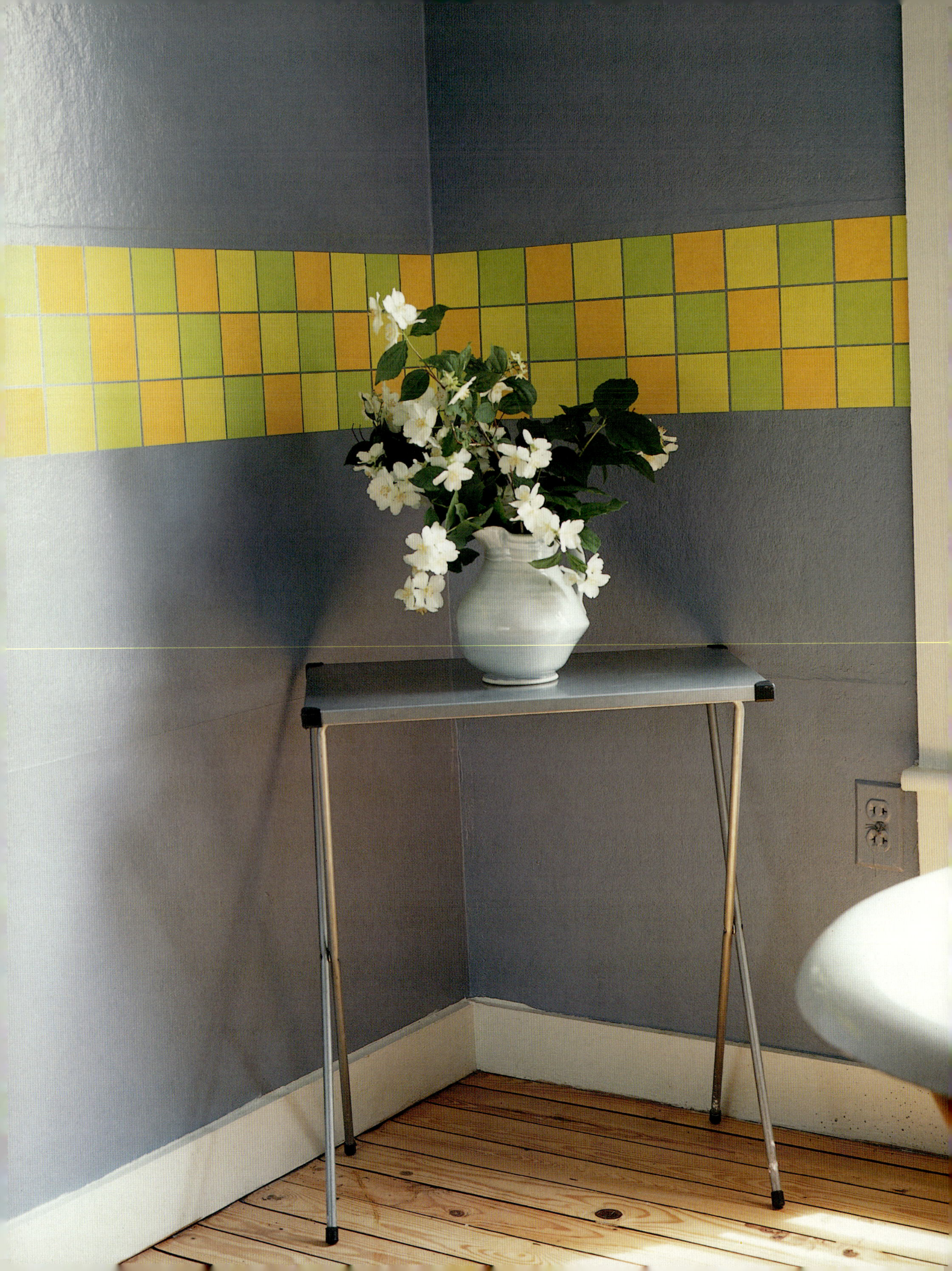

WALLS AND FLOORS

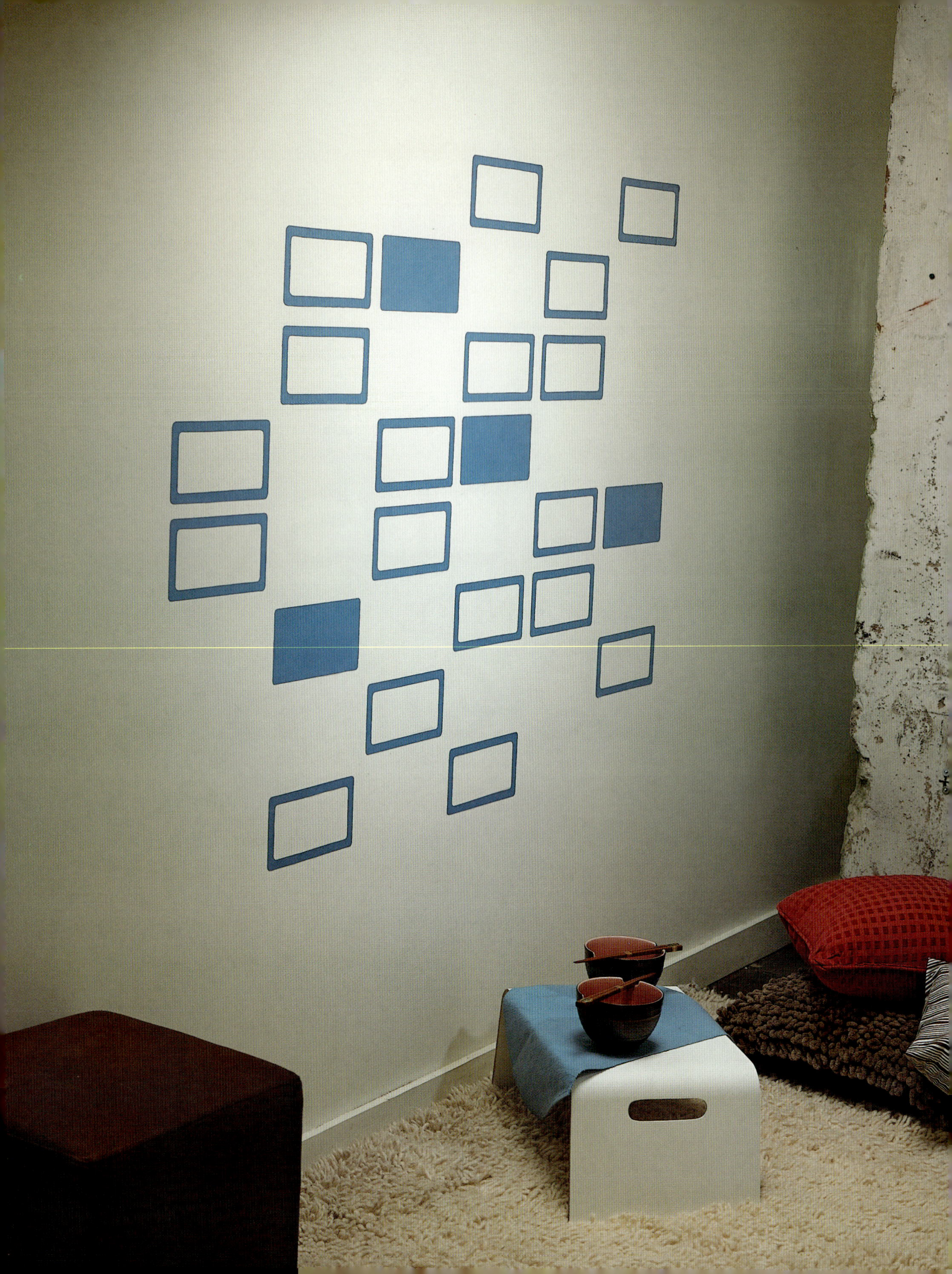

card stock wall grid

WALLS AND FLOORS

The cool sign of a now-defunct shoe store in my neighborhood inspired this design, which goes to show that great decor ideas are lurking everywhere. The simple lines and bold color make a white wall a boon, and the materials are oh so cheap. Putting lots of care into lining up the shapes perfectly will help you pull off the manufactured look.

12 sheets 8½ x 11-inch blue card stock	Scissors
L-shaped ruler	Pencil with eraser
Craft knife	Level
Self-healing cutting mat	Ball of string
	2 rolls double-sided ¼-inch tape

1. Fold each piece of card stock in half widthwise. Along the folded edge, cut off 1 inch using the ruler, craft knife, and mat. Each sheet of stock should yield two 4½ x 8½-inch rectangles. Round off the corners with scissors. Set aside four, which will be solid, not hollow.

2. On one rectangle, draw an interior rectangle ½ inch away from the edges and round off the corners. Cut out this shape and use it as a template to draw the centers of 18 hollow rectangles. Cut out the centers by slicing an X with the craft knife, then inserting the scissors to cut along the lines.

3. Make a pencil mark where you want the design's center point to fall on your wall, then use the level to draw two perpendicular lines through this point. The vertical line should be 45 inches, the horizontal line 60 inches.

4. Make a grid with string to guide your placement of each rectangle. Cut five lengths of string to 45 inches. Place one string on the vertical pencil line

WALLS AND FLOORS

and tape down its ends. Use the L-shaped ruler to mark two dots that, when connected by another string, will form a parallel line 9½ inches away. Tape a string in place, mark for another parallel line 9½ inches away, and repeat until you have placed all the 45-inch strings on either side of the vertical center line. Repeat this process on the horizontal with the 60-inch strings, making the parallel lines 5½ inches apart. (See figure 11.)

5. Put double-sided tape on a few rectangles at a time. Place them in the string grid according to the pictured design, centering each one in its cell (there should be ½ inch of space between a rectangle's edges and the string).

6. Remove the string and erase the pencil marks.

If you're a hasty type and don't mind a wall that looks like the other kids', you can purchase removable decals instead of making your own from card stock.

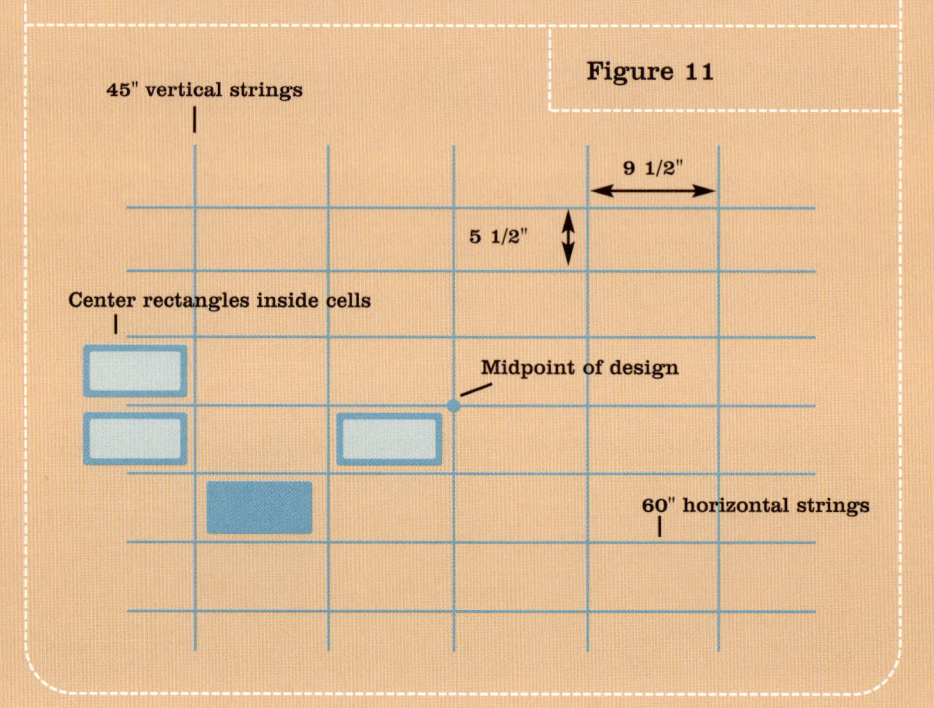

Figure 11

45" vertical strings

9 1/2"

5 1/2"

Center rectangles inside cells

Midpoint of design

60" horizontal strings

domino backsplash

WALLS AND FLOORS

Sometimes the drollest objects become pleasingly mod when assembled en masse. The dominoes' dancing pips remind me of a computer's circuitry or a spaceship's blinking switchboard. The plastic game pieces are as shiny and uniform as ceramic tile but—huge bonus—don't require grouting. Best of all, the whole backsplash hangs on the wall like a picture, so you can take it with you if you move.

Newspaper
3/4-inch plywood cut to 14 x 24 inches at your hardware store
Bricks or other items for elevating wood
Gloss black spray paint
Ruler
Hammer
2 ring hangers with nails for attaching to the plywood
Hot glue gun and glue sticks
6 sets standard-size plastic dominoes (24 pieces per set)
Flathead screwdriver
Tape
2 picture hangers with nails

1. Outdoors or in a well-ventilated area, cover a work surface with newspaper. Elevate the plywood on bricks and spray paint the sides black. Let the paint dry and apply a second coat.

2. When the paint is dry, hammer in the two ring hangers on one side of the board, 2 inches down from one of the long edges. This will be the backside.

3. Turn the board over and begin hot gluing on dominoes, starting in a corner and working your way outward. Select them randomly and position them horizontally and vertically. If you misplace a piece, ply it off with the screwdriver and reglue it.

WALLS AND FLOORS

4. When you're done gluing dominoes, hang the backsplash like this: Ball up two pieces of tape, sticky side out, and stick a ball on the tip of each ring hanger. Hold the backsplash in front of the wall where you want it, and press the backside against the wall to transfer the tape from the hangers to the wall. Hammer in your picture hangers where the tape indicates, then hang.

If you want your backsplash to be a different size, here's how to figure out how many domino sets you need: Multiply the length by the width of your board to get the square inches. Divide that number by 2, since each domino measures 2 square inches. Divide that number by 28, since a set of dominoes contains 28 game pieces.

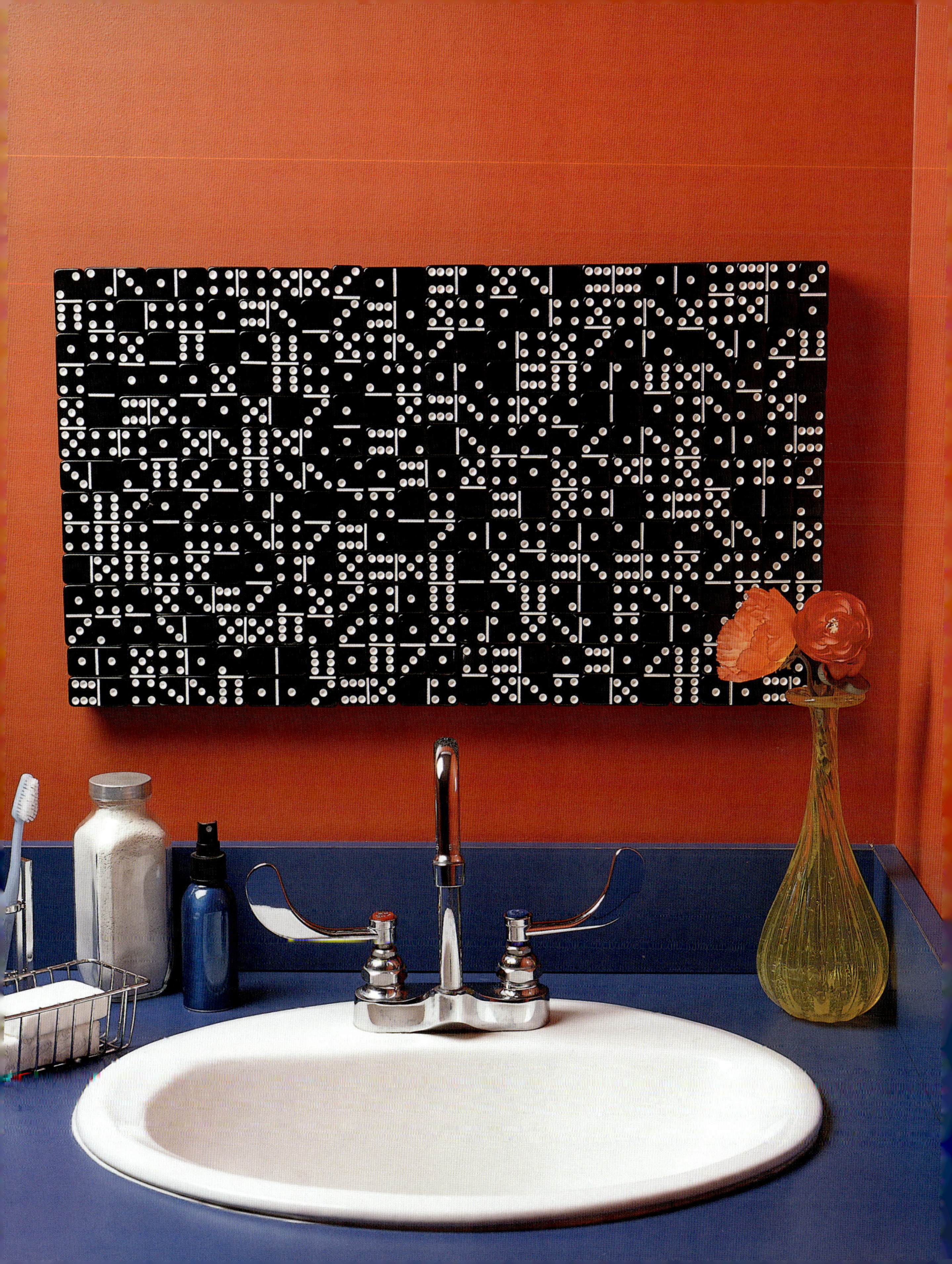

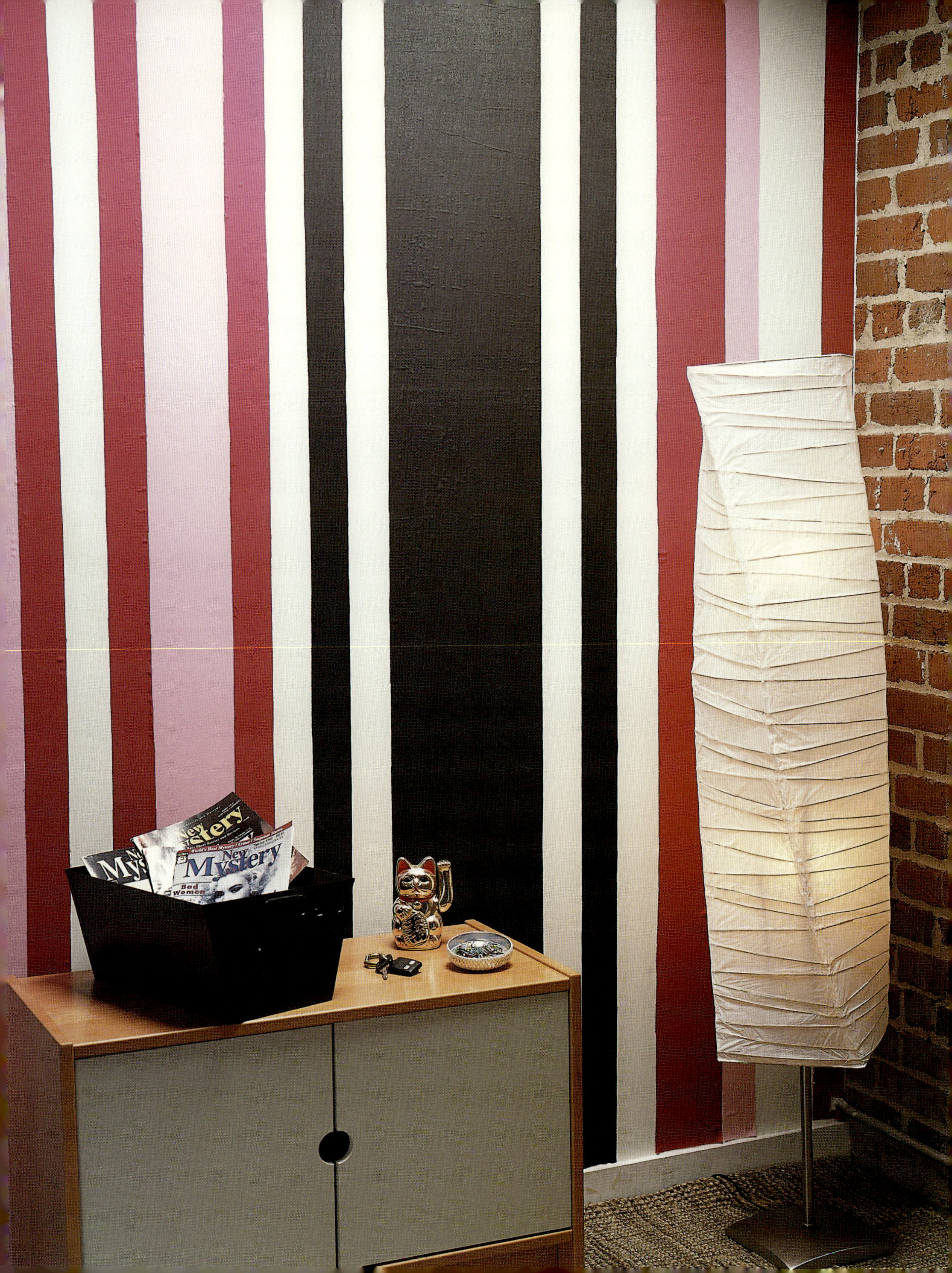

WALLS AND FLOORS

fabric-striped wall

This temporary wall treatment is not only arresting and apartment-friendly, it also demonstrates a scientific anomaly. Lightweight fabric soaked with spray starch flattens out and clings to a wall indefinitely. I suppose it works for the same reason that rice sticks to the bottom of a pot. Peel off the stripes when their time is done and wipe off any starchy residue. Your landlady will never know that her white wall hosted such colorful festooning.

Lightweight cotton fabric in light pink, dark pink, and black (buy enough yardage for your ceiling height, plus ½ yard)
Long ruler
Pencil
Self-healing cutting mat
Rotary cutter
Stepladder
Tacks
2 or more cans heavy-duty spray starch

---

1. Wash and dry the fabrics to preshrink them and set their dye.

2. Lay out each fabric panel on the floor and use the ruler and pencil to draw cutting lines for the stripes. I used widths of 3, 6, and 9 inches. Place the mat beneath the fabric at one end and make the cuts with the ruler and rotary cutter. Pause and move the mat along as needed.

3. Give yourself guidelines for hanging the stripes parallel by measuring and making pencil marks just below the ceiling or crown molding and just above the baseboard or floor. Don't forget to mark for white stripes.

4. Stand on the stepladder and line up a stripe with its marks, allowing excess fabric at the top and bottom. Place two tacks through the fabric just below the ceiling. Hang all the stripes in this way. For stripes that butt, overlap the darker fabric slightly.

5. Begin spraying starch onto a stripe's upper area. Thoroughly soak the fabric and smooth it against the wall with your hand. Have a friend sit on the floor below and hold the bottom of the fabric in the appropriate place while you spray and smooth. Continue in this way with all the stripes.

6. Let the starch dry, then remove the tacks. Use the rotary cutter to trim the stripes' tops and bottoms. Trim any frayed edges as well.

WALLS AND FLOORS

memo pad mosaic border

Give yourself a more worthwhile reason for stealing office supplies from work. Those sticky memo notes are the perfect size to pose as tiles in a kitchen or bathroom that's lacking in architectural details, and they add a shock of color without painting. Clear shelf liner keeps the notes dry and flat. This technique eats so little time and money that you can change it often or cover a whole wall, if the supply closet allows.

Pencil	Newspaper
Level	Spray adhesive
Long ruler	Clear adhesive-backed shelf liner
Sticky memo pads in three colors	Scissors

1. Use the pencil, level, and ruler to draw a horizontal line on the wall, under which to set the top row of notes.

2. Decide what pattern, if any, you want for the notes. I kept the colors in order throughout but varied which color started each row. The top goes A, B, C; the middle, B, C, A; and the bottom, C, A, B.

3. Spread out lots of newspaper and open the windows for ventilation. Remove your first note from the pad, put it sticky side up on the newspaper, spray it with adhesive, and smooth it onto the wall below the pencil line. For the next color, set it in a different place on the newspaper to keep the note's front side clean. Place it on the wall, leaving about $1/16$ inch between the notes to act as a "grout line." Repeat until the border is complete. Leave $1/16$ inch between the rows as well.

WALLS AND FLOORS

4. Roll out and cut enough shelf liner to cover the length of your design. Use the long ruler, pencil, and scissors to cut the width down to 10 inches, if you have three rows of notes. Peel off the backing and smooth the liner over the border.

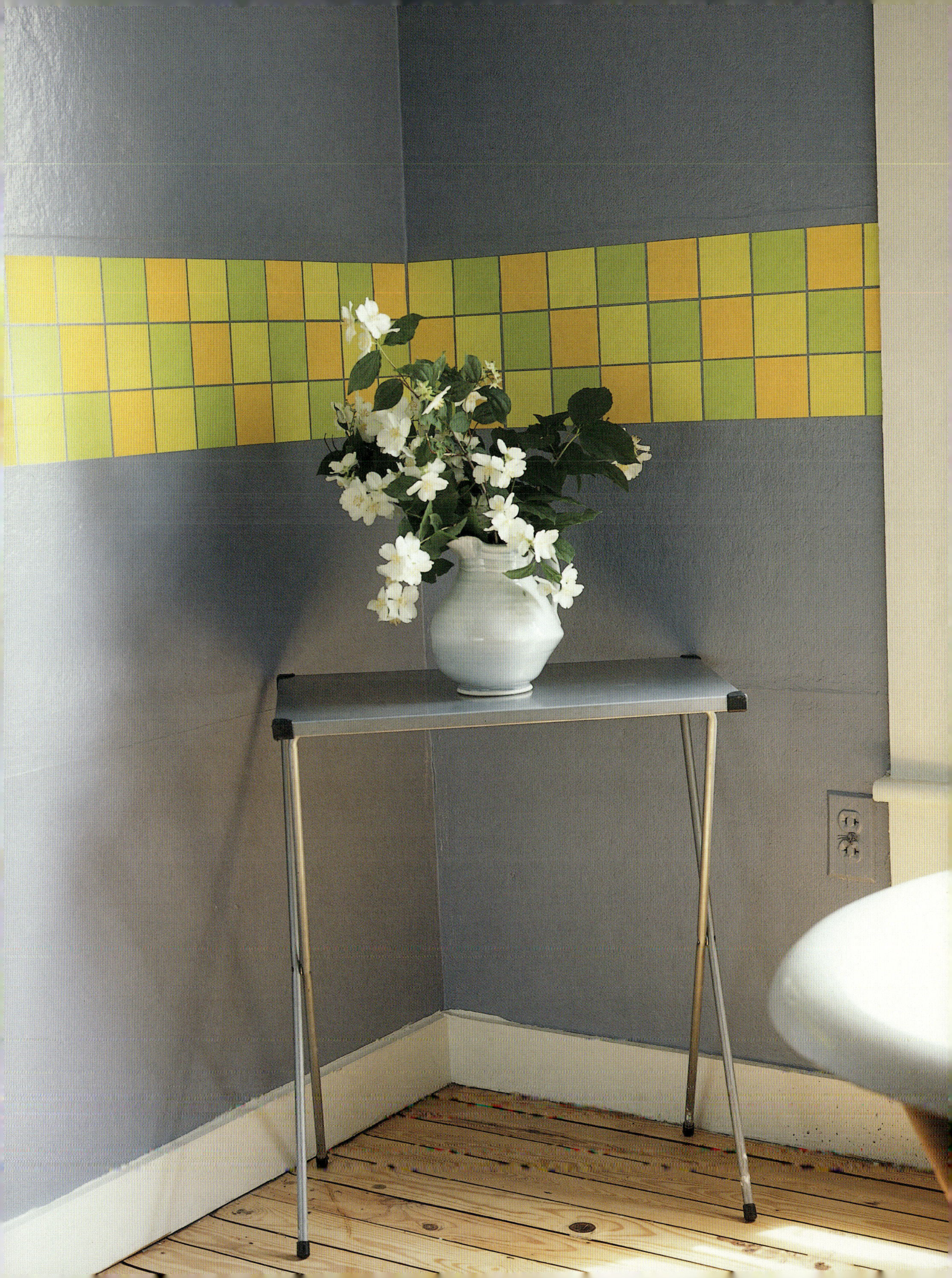

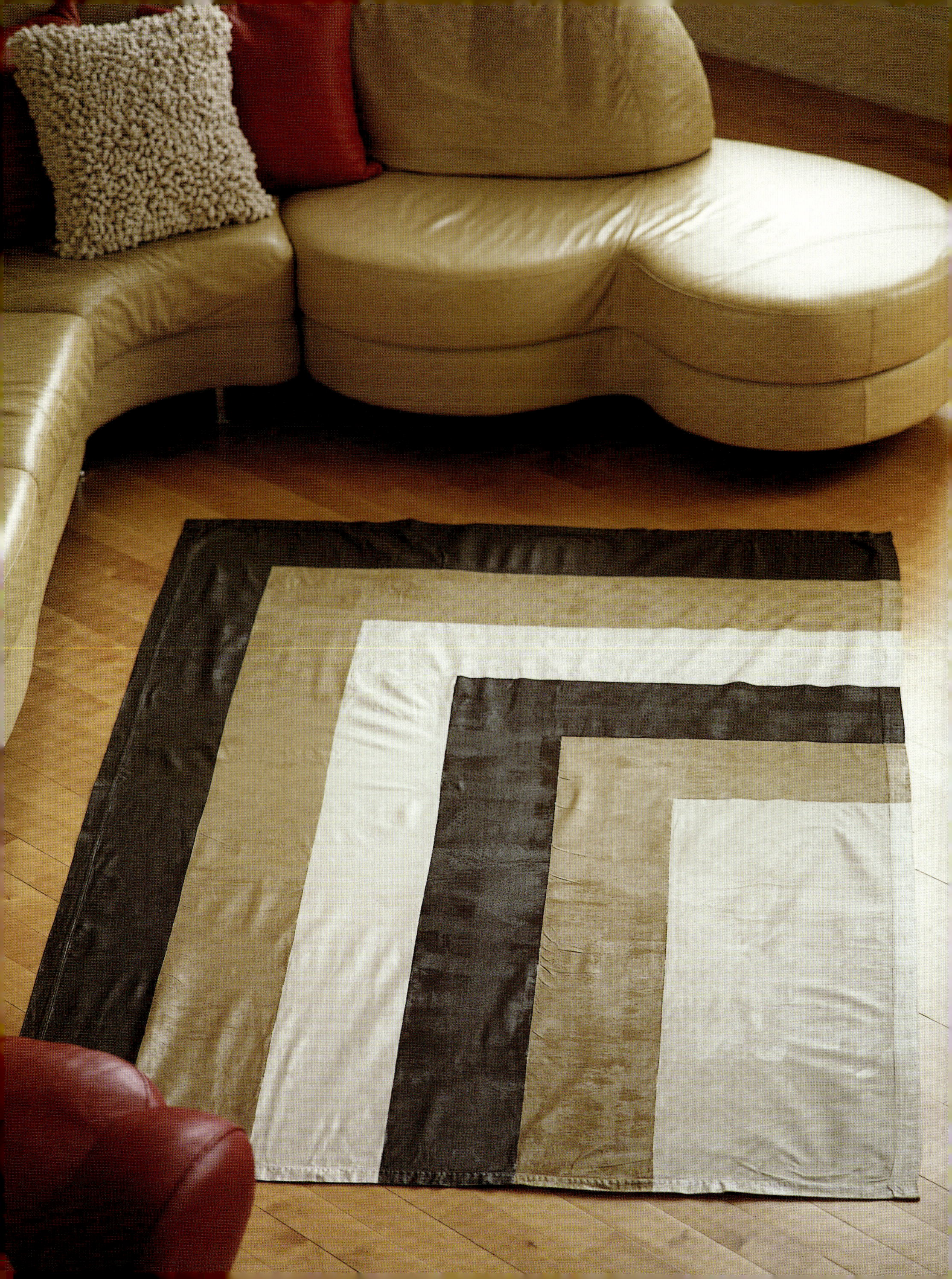

WALLS AND FLOORS

painted floorcloth

Ever notice that contemporary rugs cost about ten times as much as their Victorian floral counterparts? Until the marketplace catches on to our tastes, we've got to take decorating into our own hands. Using a tablecloth and latex paint is an easy way to get some clean lines underfoot without requesting an advance on your paycheck. You can create countless patterns with a ruler and masking tape. Don't skimp on paint: the cotton cloth is thirsty and will require at least two coats, plus touchups.

Plastic drop cloth
60 x 90-inch 100 percent cotton tablecloth or drop cloth
Large T-shaped ruler
Pencil
3-inch-wide masking tape
Craft knife
1 quart each off-white, light brown, and dark brown interior latex paint
Small paint tray
Mini foam roller
Aluminum foil
Foam paintbrush
1 quart acrylic sealer

---

1. Use the plastic drop cloth to protect your floor while you work. Lay out the tablecloth and place the crossbar of the T-shaped ruler even with one of the long edges. Use the pencil to make a mark on the cloth at 8, 16, 24, 32, and 40 inches. Move the ruler over a couple of feet and repeat these marks.

2. Place the crossbar of the ruler along one of the cloth's short edges and repeat these two sets of marks.

3. Line up the long part of the ruler with each of the twin sets of marks and draw a pencil line from one end of the cloth to the other. You'll end up with a grid of perpendicular lines you'll use to tape off L-shaped stripes.

4. You can't paint more than one color at a time since they all touch, so begin by taping off only the two white stripes. You may have to use the craft knife to remove some tape at inside corners to make 90-degree angles. Pour white paint into the tray and roll it inside the taped areas. Let it dry, paint a second coat, then remove the tape. (Tip: While you're waiting for the first coat to dry, wrap the wet roller in foil to keep it moist.) Wash the roller and tray.

5. When the white stripes are dry, tape off and paint the light brown stripes. Remove the tape after two coats and wash the roller and tray.

6. When the light brown stripes are dry, tape off and paint the dark brown stripes. Remove the tape after two coats and wash the roller and tray.

7. Use the foam brush for touchup work. Wash the brush before you change colors.

8. When the whole cloth is dry, roll on the acrylic sealer. Let it dry and apply a second coat.

When you want to store the floorcloth, roll it painted-side-out around a dowel or pipe.

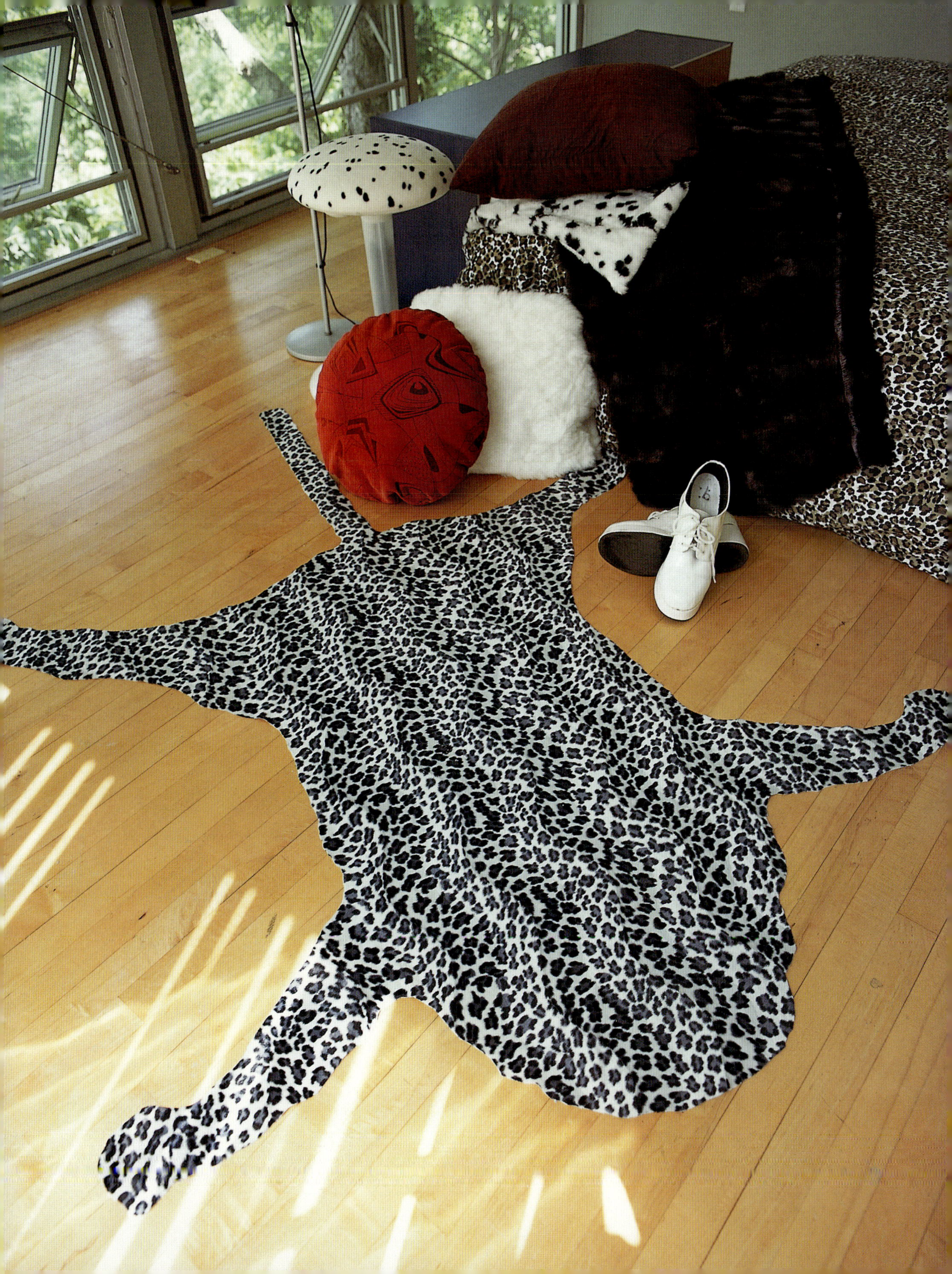

WALLS AND FLOORS

faux leopard rug

Animal prints have lots of associations—Hemingway, harems, 1970s playboy mansions—that can add some tongue-in-cheek fun to your dwelling. Real skins are rare and expensive, however, so hunt down a couple of yards of faux fur and spare the earth's beasts their hides.

---

2 yards leopard faux fur, 60 inches wide
Pencil
Long ruler

Straight pins
Scissors
Repositionable rug tape or light-duty carpet tape (optional)

---

1. Fold the fabric in half lengthwise with the wrong side up. The folded edge will be the center of the hide, so you need to draw only half of its outline. Use the pencil and ruler to sketch the leopard's shape as shown in the diagram. (See figure 12.)

2. Pin together the fabric layers along the edges to keep them from shifting. Cut out the shape, using jagged and choppy movements to imitate an authentic pelt.

3. Hold the rug in place on the floor with rug tape if you like.

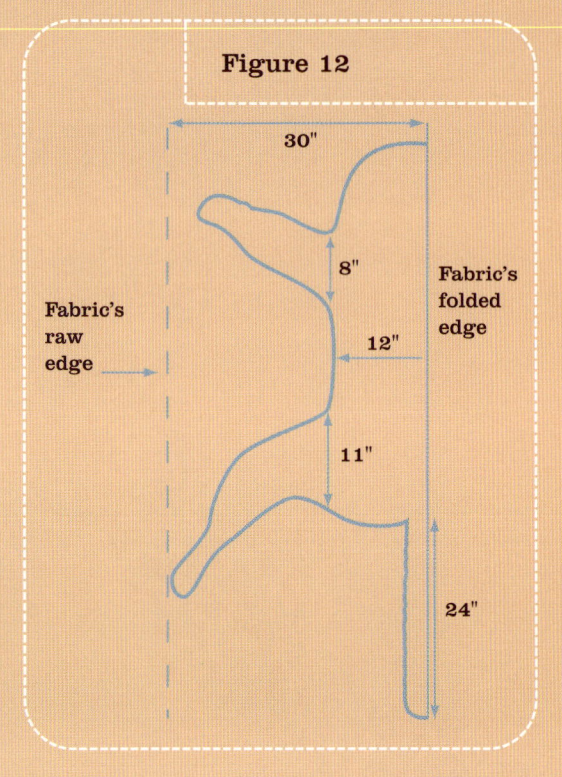

Figure 12

30"
8"
Fabric's raw edge
12"
Fabric's folded edge
11"
24"

130

inlaid faux fur rug

WALLS AND FLOORS

I have a weakness for area rugs, but I'd be decorating in the poorhouse if I bought them as often as I'd like. Faux fur is an inexpensive alternative that feels fuzzy on the feet and comes in many colors and textures. Inlaying two colors offers endless pattern possibilities, and rug tape secures your unique pelt to the floor. The directions are for a 4 x 6-foot rug; adjust the fabric yardage as necessary if you want a different size.

---

2 yards 45-inch-wide textured pink fur
L-shaped ruler
Marker
Scissors
Cardboard
Round coaster or other small circular object

Utility knife
Self-healing cutting mat
$3/4$ yard white fur
Repositionable rug tape or light-duty carpet tape

---

1. If the finished edges of the pink fur look nice, leave them as is. Turn the fabric wrong side up and mark the two cut ends using the L-shaped ruler and marker to ensure that the corners are square. Cut along the lines.

2. Make your flower template by placing the coaster on the cardboard and drawing boxy petals around it. My flower's diameter is 13 inches. Each petal should touch its neighbors at the base. Some petal variation adds character, so don't be too perfect. Cut out the template using the utility knife and mat.

3. Trace around the template six times on the backside of the white fur. Cut out the flowers.

4. Place the flowers on the backside of the pink fur to determine your arrangement. Mark dots around each flower to indicate where to place the template.

WALLS AND FLOORS

Trace around the template inside each dotted circle, then cut out the flower shapes. Begin each cut by folding the fabric inside the shape and making a slit along the fold.

5. Shake off any excess fur from both fabrics, then bring them to the desired location. Place the pink fur right side up where you want it, then turn over the edges one at a time and line them with rug tape. Remove the paper liner and press the fabric to the floor. Place the white flowers on the pink fur, turn up the petals, line them with tape, and press them down. Tape the triangular pieces of pink fur between the white petals as well.

- If an area of the rug will experience stress, such as a door opening or a chair sliding, place extra tape there.

- To clean the rug, go over it gently with a handheld vacuum.

- When you're ready to remove the rug and tape, clean off any tape residue on the floor with denatured alcohol.

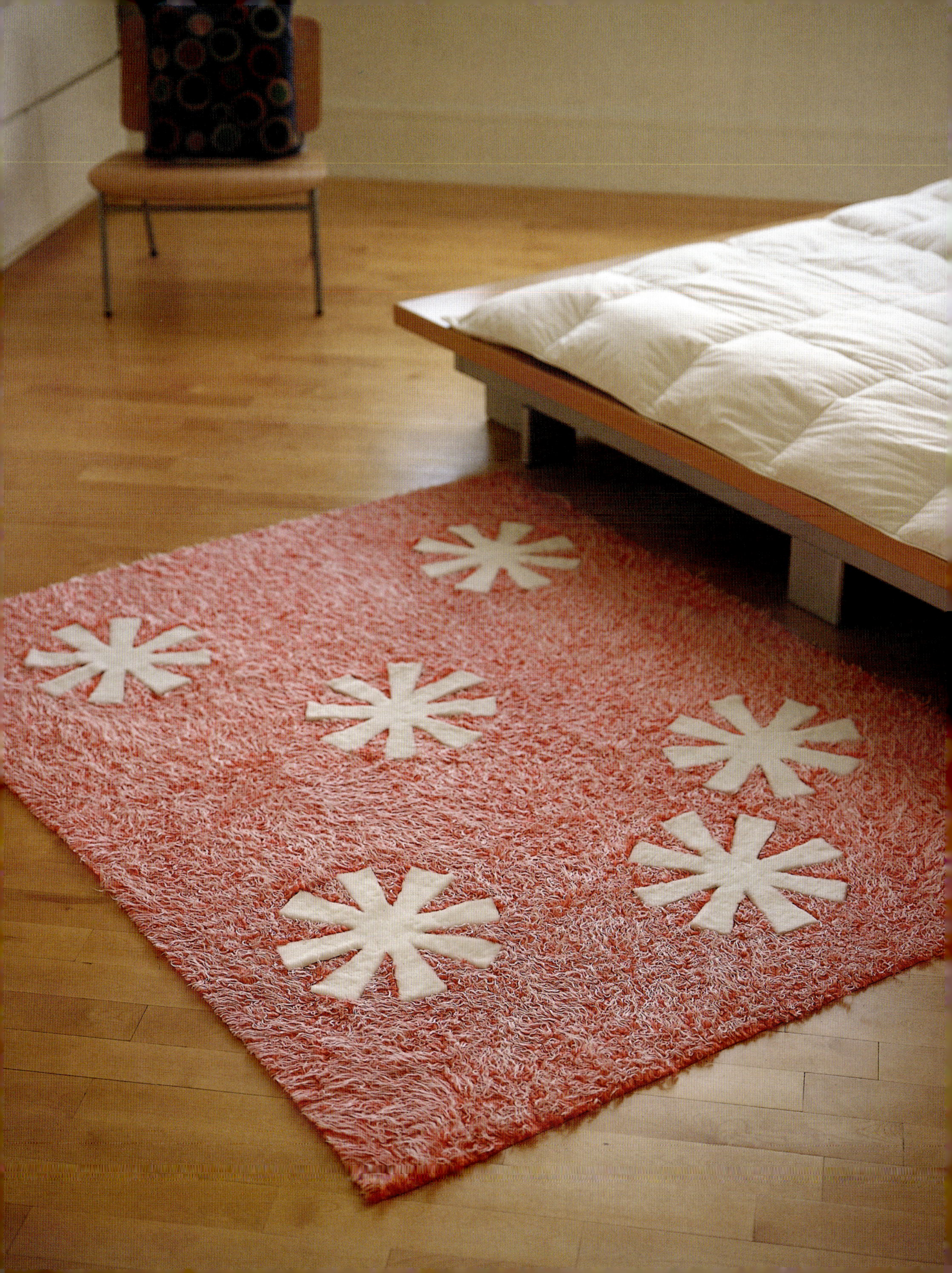

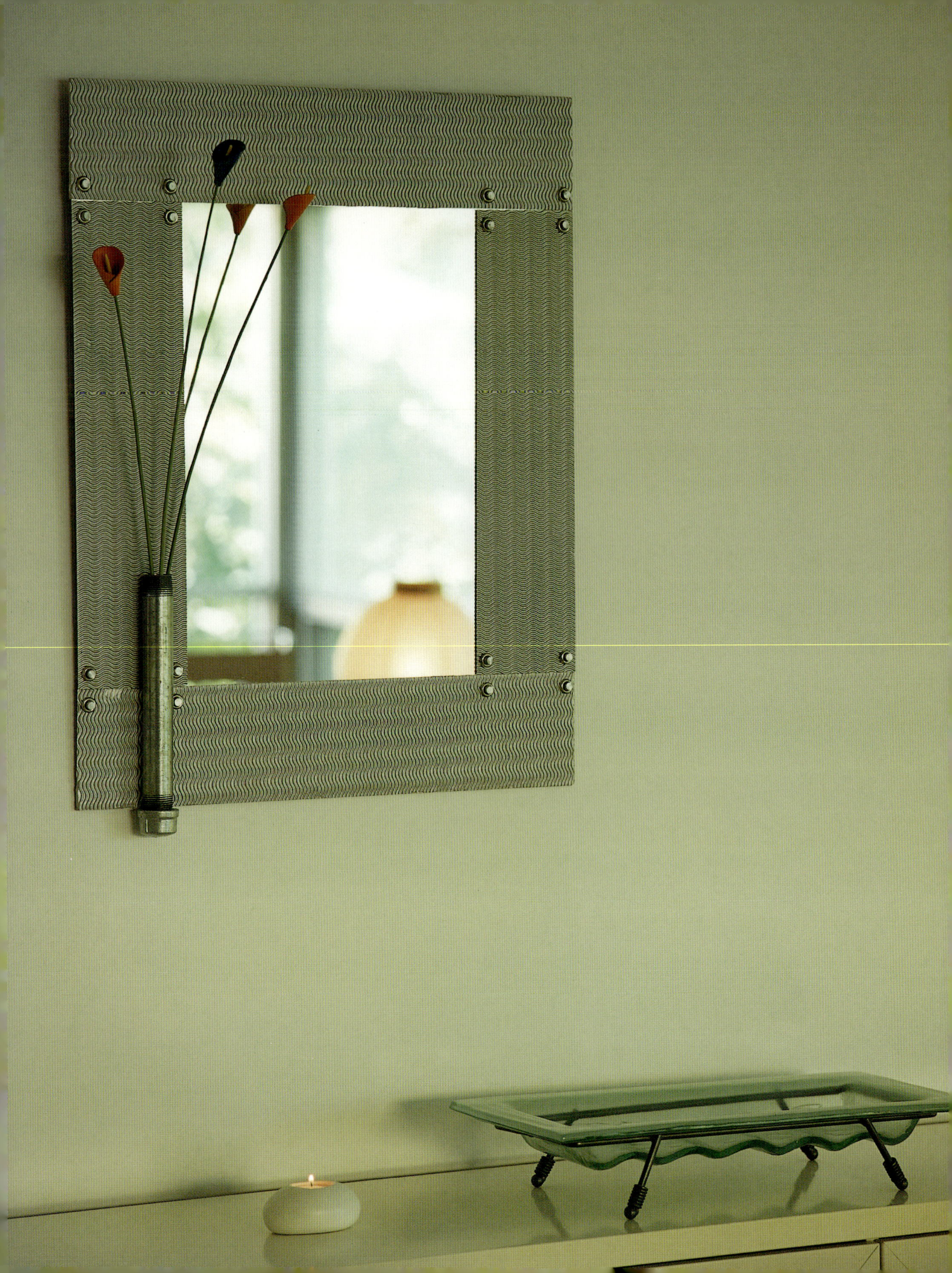

ACCESSORIES

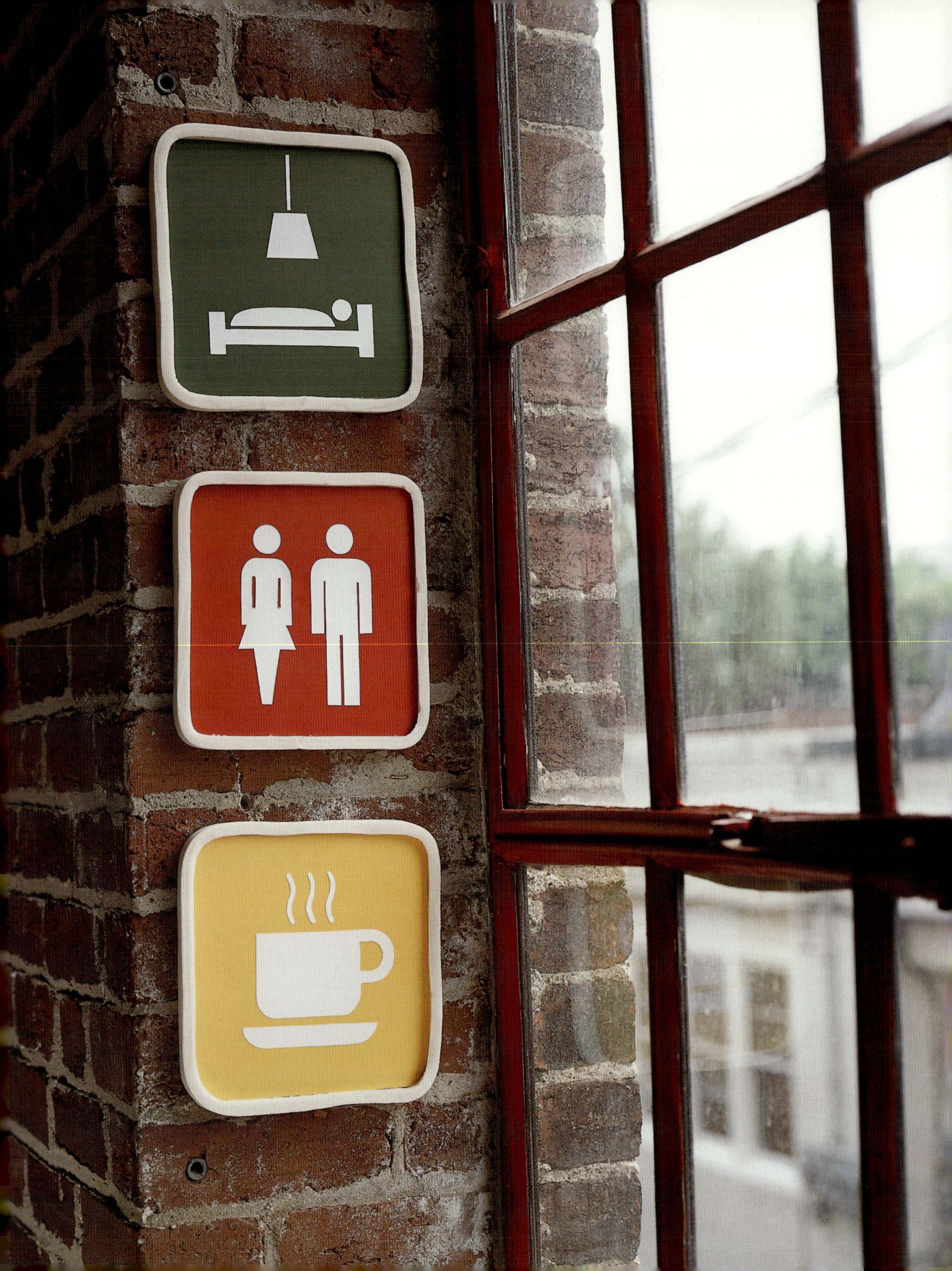

ACCESSORIES

household icons

Are you plagued by houseguests who mistake the kitchen for the bathroom, the powder room for the boudoir? Clear up the confusion with these snappy icons inspired by a road trip and assembled from clip art, colorful foam boards, and card stock. Weather-stripping foam, which usually trims doors and windows in winter, moonlights as a decorative border that delivers an authentic highway feel. If you like, personalize your images with additions, such as a hanging light for the bedroom sign.

Ruler
Utility knife
Self-healing cutting mat
1 each red, yellow, and green foam board
Clip-art images like those shown (many are available on the Internet; use the key words **restroom**, **coffee**, and **lodging** when you're searching)
3 sheets white card stock
Scissors
Foam paintbrush
Craft glue
At least 7 feet white weather-stripping foam
Hot glue gun and glue sticks
Large rubber bands
Adhesive mounting squares

1. With the ruler, utility knife, and mat, cut a 7-inch square from each color of foam board.

2. On a copier, enlarge your clip-art images if necessary. Print them on white card stock. Cut them out with scissors and use the utility knife for any interior cuts. If you like, cut out additional pieces from the card stock, such as a ceiling fixture.

3. Brush the ink side of each clip-art cutout with craft glue and glue it to a foam board.

ACCESSORIES

4. Secure one end of the weather-stripping foam to the bottom edge of a sign with a dot of hot glue. Squeeze on a few inches of craft glue, press the trim down, then add another dot of hot glue to hold it in place. Continue in this way around the sign, cut off the excess trim, and finish with a dot of hot glue. (Do not use hot glue all the way around. You'll risk burning the foam core of the sign and the weather-stripping foam with the glue gun's hot tip.) If needed, put rubber bands on the signs to hold the trim flush while the glue dries.

5. Attach the mounting squares to the signs' backs and hang them.

sunny atomic clock

ACCESSORIES

Is it a sunburst? A building block of matter? It's a little of both, and not at all difficult to make. And the cost? I've bought toiletries that set me back twice as much. Plus, you'll learn a trick in this project applicable to many others involving spray painting: when you need to paint wily three-dimensional objects such as foam balls, skewer them and stick them into scrap foam so that you can reach all sides as you spray.

Pencil
Small plate (mine has a 5½-inch diameter) for tracing your clock face
3/16-inch-thick foam board
Self-healing cutting mat
Craft knife
Scissors
Nail file
Awl

Clock movement and hands (the movement should be designated for ¼-inch surfaces)
Twelve 1½-inch Styrofoam balls
Package of 6-inch bamboo skewers
Scrap packing foam
Newspaper
Matte spray paint in yellow and black
Craft glue
Battery

1. To make the clock face, trace the plate on the foam board. Place the mat under your drawing and slowly score the line with the craft knife as follows: insert the point, tilt the sharp side down to slice along the line a little, pull out the blade, and insert it at the next spot. After scoring the circle, go back over the line in one smooth motion, pressing down on the knife to cut all the way through the foam board.

2. Even if you cut carefully, your circle may have some jagged edges. Trim off any large bits with scissors, then fine-tune the edges with the nail file.

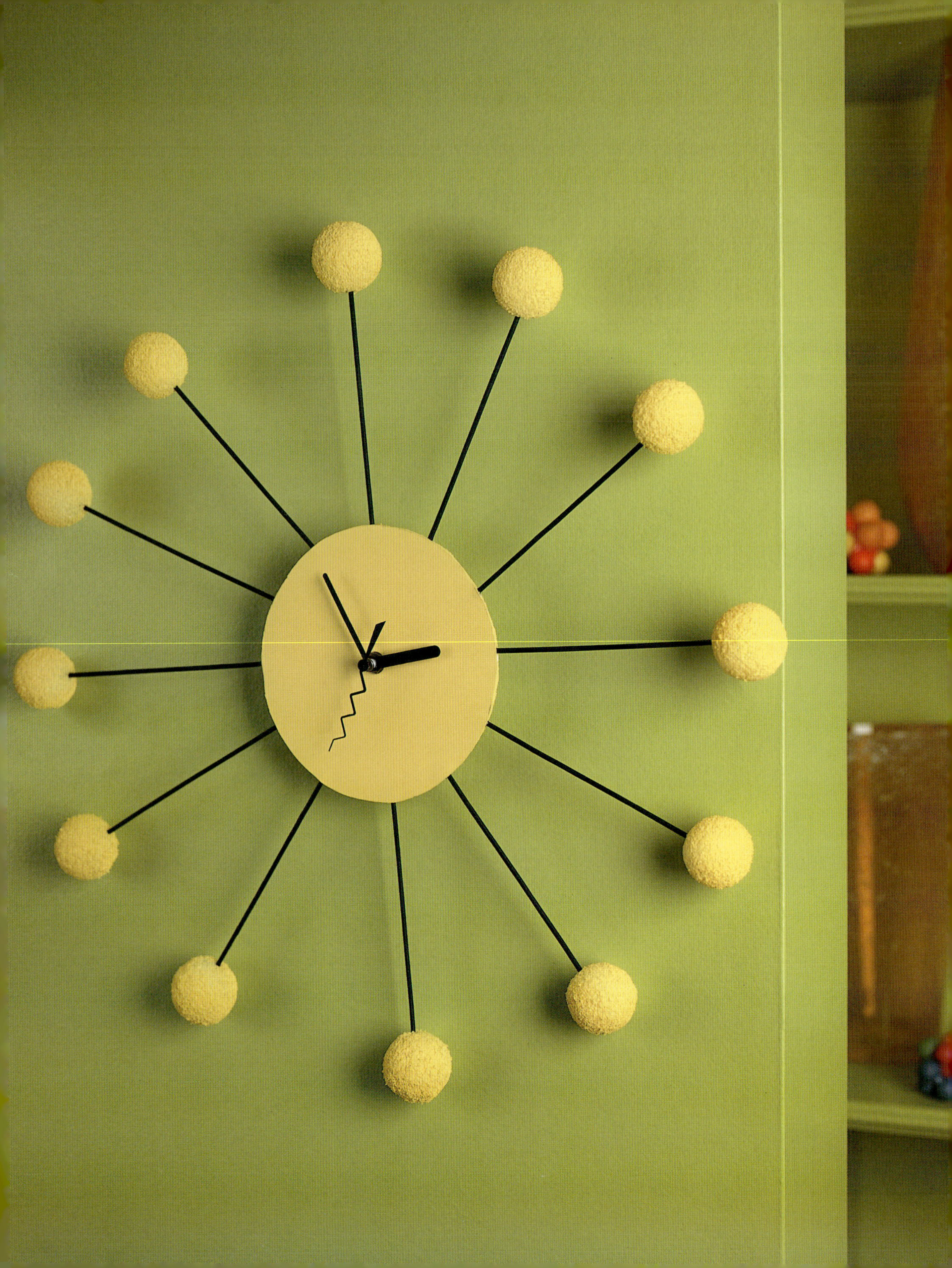

ACCESSORIES

3. Designate the more pristine side as the front and mark the circle's midpoint on the back. Use the awl to slowly punch a hole large enough for the threaded shaft of the clock movement.

4. Pierce a foam ball with a skewer and stick its other end in the scrap foam. Repeat with all the remaining balls. Take the scrap foam and mounted balls outside or to a well-ventilated area, spread newspaper over your work surface, and spray paint the balls yellow. Spray the clock's face and sides yellow as well.

5. Insert at least 12 skewers into another piece of scrap foam (you may want to paint a few extra in case any become bent or splintered). Spray paint them black. If the clock hands aren't already black, put them on newspaper and paint them too.

6. When all your painted parts are dry, assemble the clock movement components on the clock face according to the manufacturer's instructions. Make light pencil marks on the foam board's core where the black skewers should go (they represent the hours). Put a dab of glue on both ends of a skewer, insert the flat end into the existing hole in a yellow ball, and insert the pointed end into the foam board's core. Repeat for the remaining rays.

7. Let the glue dry, then pop in a battery, hang your clock, and set the time.

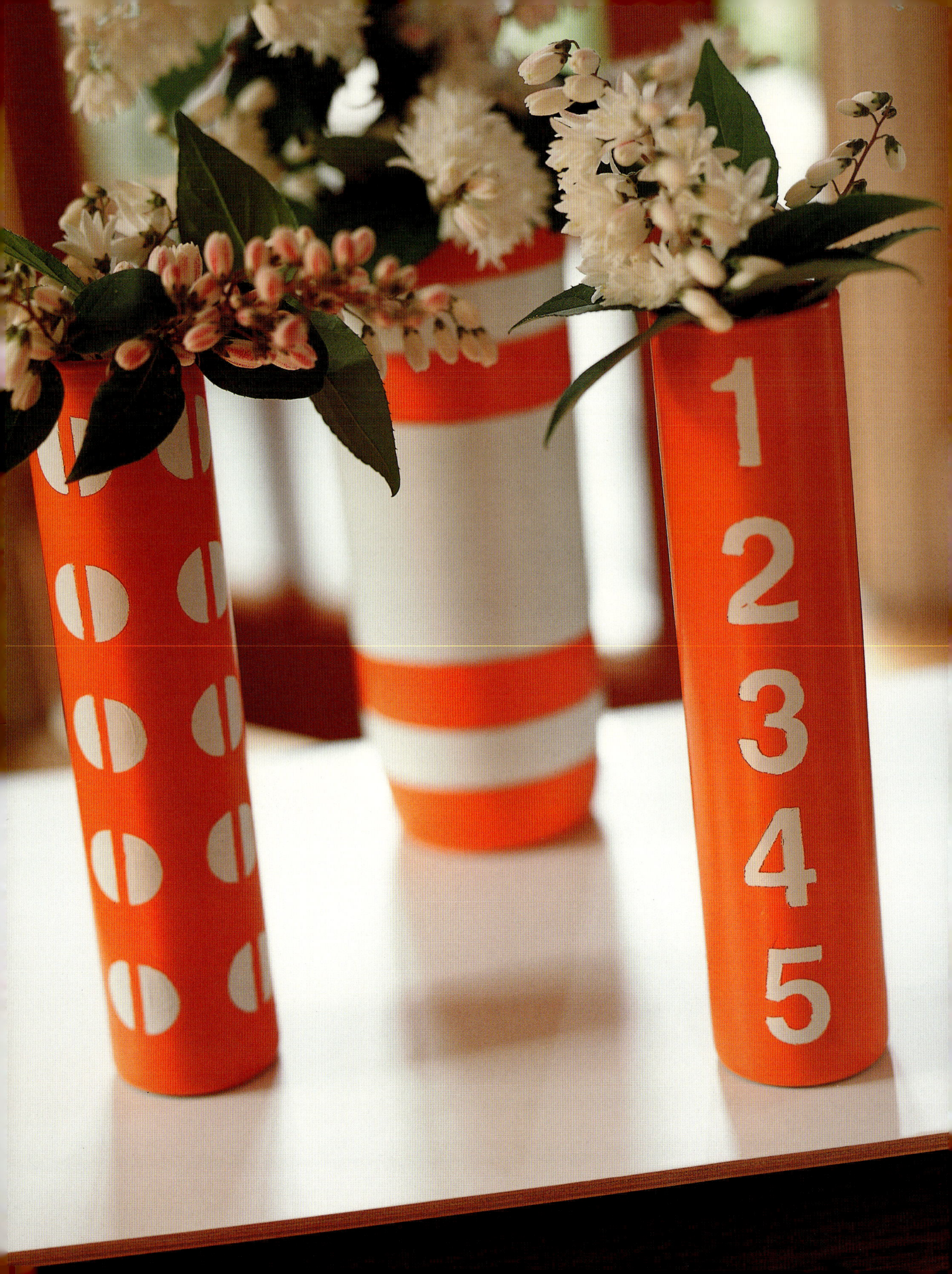
1
2
3
4
5

ACCESSORIES

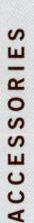

spray-painted bud vases

You can spray paint on glass with household paint if you start with an oil-based primer, which sticks to even the slickest surface. Painter's tape and stickers offer lots of masking possibilities, and you can also create one-of-a-kind designs by cutting custom shapes out of large sticky labels.

3 glass bud vases
Rubbing alcohol
Paper towels
Newspaper
Oil-based spray primer
Glossy white spray paint

$3/4$- and 3-inch-wide painter's tape
Round and numeric stickers
Glossy orange spray paint
Disposable plastic containers
Small artist's brushes

1. Work outdoors or in a well-ventilated area. Clean the vases with alcohol and paper towels to help the primer stick. Protect your work surface with newspaper.

2. Spray the vases with a coat of primer, let it dry, and apply a second coat. Put the vases aside for several hours to allow the primer to form a strong bond with the glass then spray with white paint. Let it dry.

3. For the striped vase, mask off the stripes with the two tape sizes. For the dotted vase, cut the round stickers in half while they're still on the backing. Place the cut halves on the vase with a small space between them, keeping equal space between the circles all around. For the numbered vase, position number stickers 1–5 in a vertical row.

4. Spray the vases orange. Let them dry, then carefully remove the tape and stickers. Spray paint into the plastic containers and use the artist's brushes to touch up any ragged areas.

ACCESSORIES

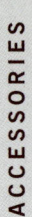

plastic mesh coasters

Remember those "Bless this house" ornaments that your grandma made for the holiday tree? She used plastic mesh rounds to anchor her cross-stitching, but they're also the perfect size to cushion a cocktail. Monochromatic spray paint and a simple template make for smart coasters that you can paint over again, whenever your mood swings. Plastic mesh comes in large rectangles, too, if you hanker for matching place mats.

Permanent marker
Four 4-inch round plastic mesh canvases
Template plastic
Scissors
Newspaper
Spray paint in light and dark blue
Repositionable spray adhesive

1. Use the marker to trace one of the coasters on the template plastic. Place all four coasters on top of the traced circle so that they are touching each other and creating a four-pointed star in the center of the traced circle. Trace around the parts of the coasters that are inside the circle.

2. Cut out the star shape, trace it three times on the plastic, and cut out the new stars.

3. Working outdoors or in a well-ventilated area, cover your work surface with newspaper. Spray paint the coasters light blue, then let them dry.

4. Spray repositionable adhesive on one side of each of the four plastic stars, then press one in the center of each coaster. Spray paint the coasters dark blue. Let the paint dry, then carefully peel off the templates.

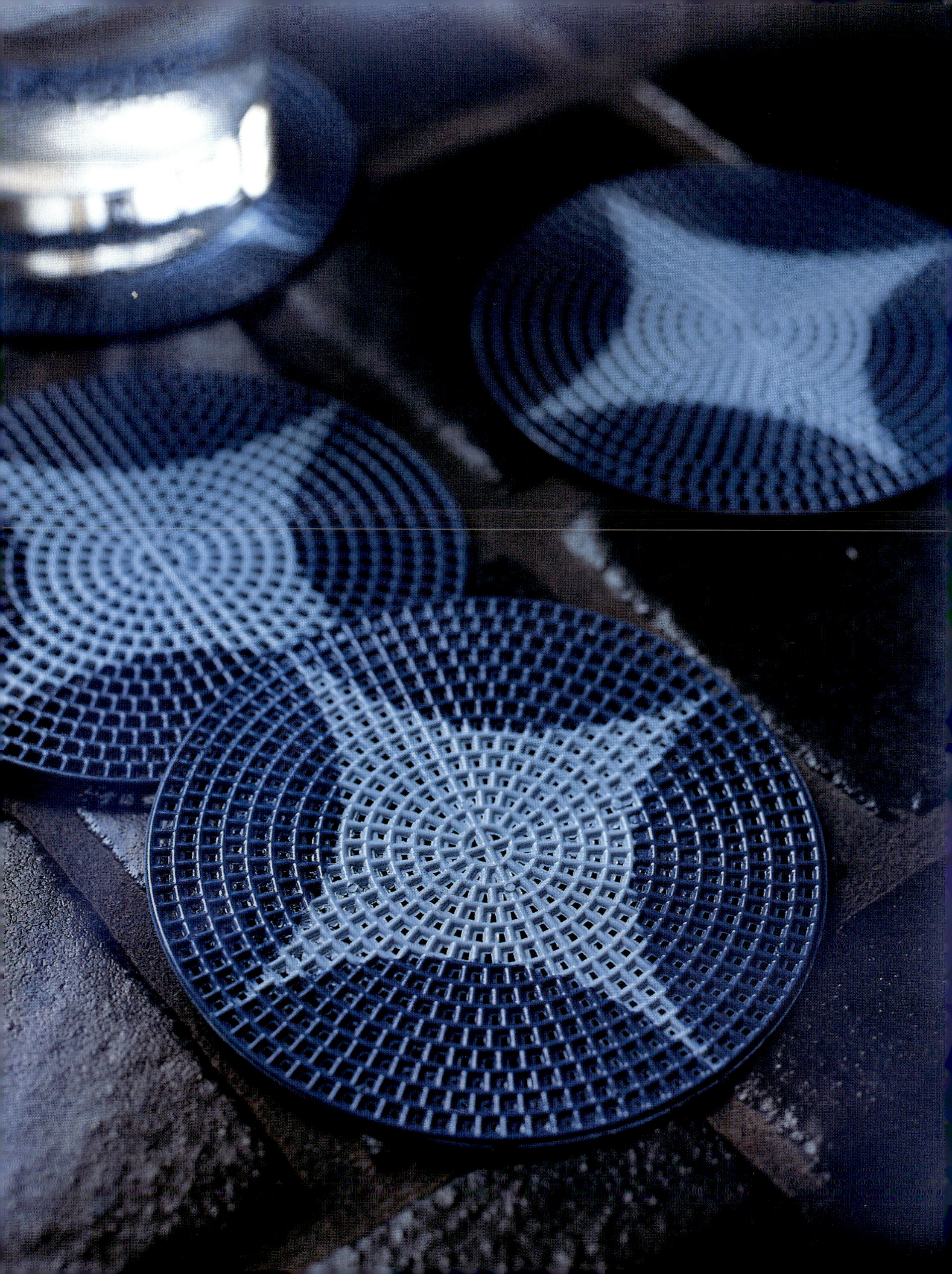

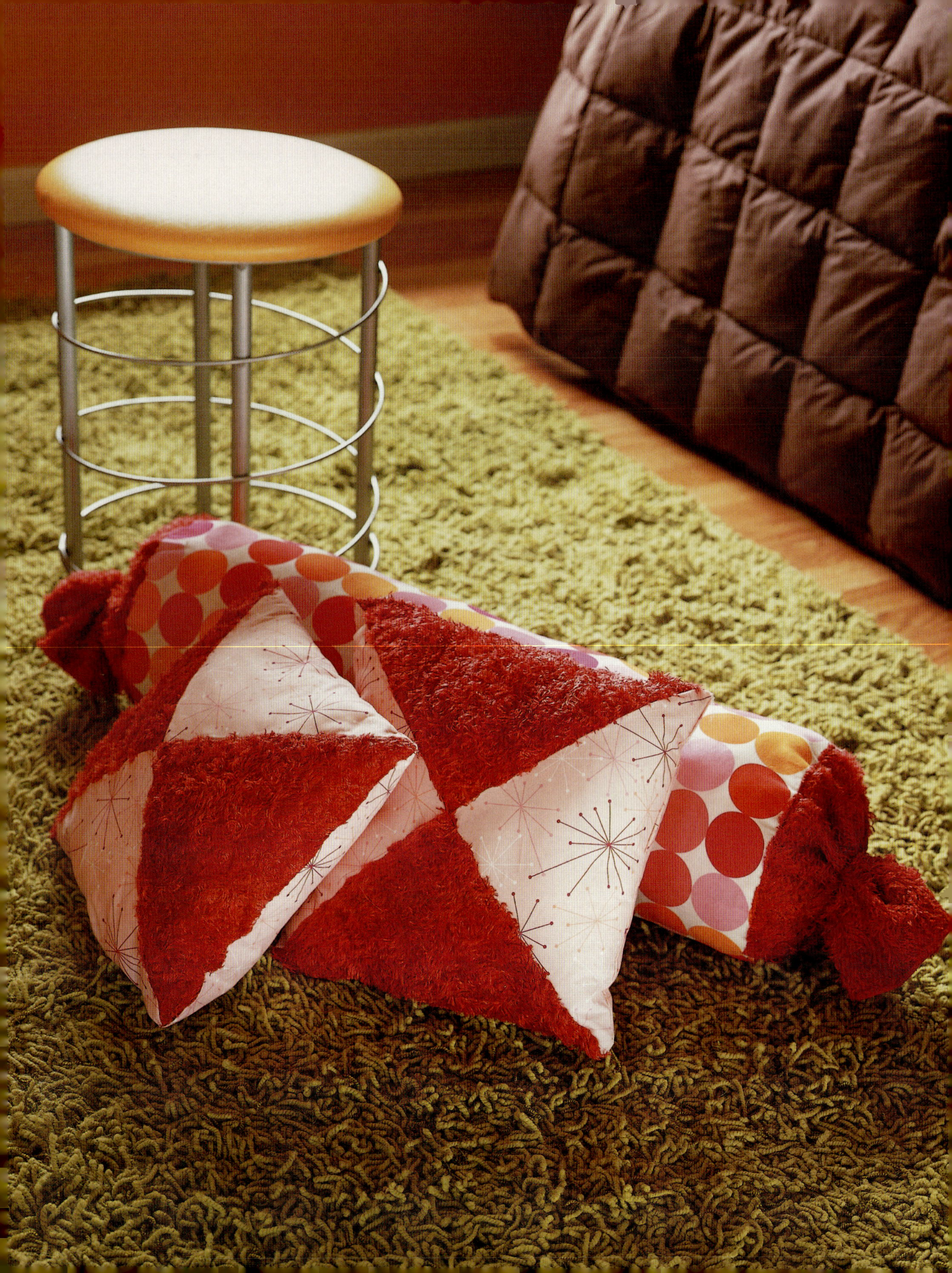

ACCESSORIES

mostly no-sew pillows

Throw pillows make your decorating mood swings bearable for your wallet. Instead of changing hefty items like sofas and chairs, just toss on some fluffy new accents you whipped up in an afternoon. The square pillows require just a few inches of hand-sewing, while the stitch-free bolster uses rubber bands to cinch it like a piece of candy.

FOR THE SQUARE PILLOWS:

- ½ yard patterned fabric
- ½ yard textured solid fabric
- Long ruler
- Scissors
- Pencil
- Iron and ironing board
- Iron-on seam tape
- Pillow filling
- Straight pins
- Needle and coordinating thread

1. Fabric-wise, it's more efficient to make two pillows than one in this case. Cut one 16-inch square from each fabric. Cut two 14-inch squares from the patterned fabric (for the pillow backs) and set these aside.

2. On the backside of the 16-inch squares, use the ruler and pencil to mark two bisecting diagonal lines. Cut out the triangles. Combine two patterned triangles and two solid ones as shown in the photo to make each pillow front.

3. Place one triangle right side up on the ironing board. Put seam tape along one of the edges where it will join with another, then place a butting triangle wrong side up on top. Follow the tape manufacturer's instructions for ironing the seam. Repeat until you have made two squares made of four triangles each.

4. Put one completed pillow front right side up on the ironing board. Cover three edges with seam tape and cover the remaining edge only halfway. Place one of the 14-inch squares wrong side up on top and iron the sides. Stick your hand in the unsealed area to turn the pillow right side out. Be sure to poke out the corners. Repeat this step for the other pillow.

5. Stuff the pillows with filling. Fold down the open seam and pin it closed. Whipstitch the seam.

HOW TO WHIPSTITCH

Thread the needle and knot the end. Pass the needle through the very top of the seam. You'll start on the same side of the pillow for every stitch. After the first and last stitches, sew backward a couple of times to lock the thread in place. Cut the thread, leaving a tail, and tie a knot after the last stitch.

ACCESSORIES

FOR THE BOLSTER PILLOW:

²/₃ yard patterned fabric
½ yard textured solid fabric
Long ruler
Scissors
Iron and ironing board

Iron-on seam tape
2 rubber bands close to the color of the solid fabric
Pillow filling

1. Cut a 24 x 26-inch piece from the patterned fabric. Cut two 8 x 24-inch pieces from the solid fabric.

2. Lay the patterned fabric right side up on the ironing board. Put seam tape along one of its 24-inch edges. Place one of the solid fabric pieces wrong side up on top, lining up the edges. Follow the tape manufacturer's instructions for ironing the seam. Repeat on the other 24-inch edge of the patterned fabric.

3. With the completed panel right side up, put seam tape along one of the edges that is now 34 inches. Fold up the opposite edge and iron the seam. Turn the tube right side out.

4. Gather one of the solid pieces in the middle and cinch it with a rubber band. Stuff the pillow from the open end. Cinch the open end with a rubber band once the pillow is full and even all around.

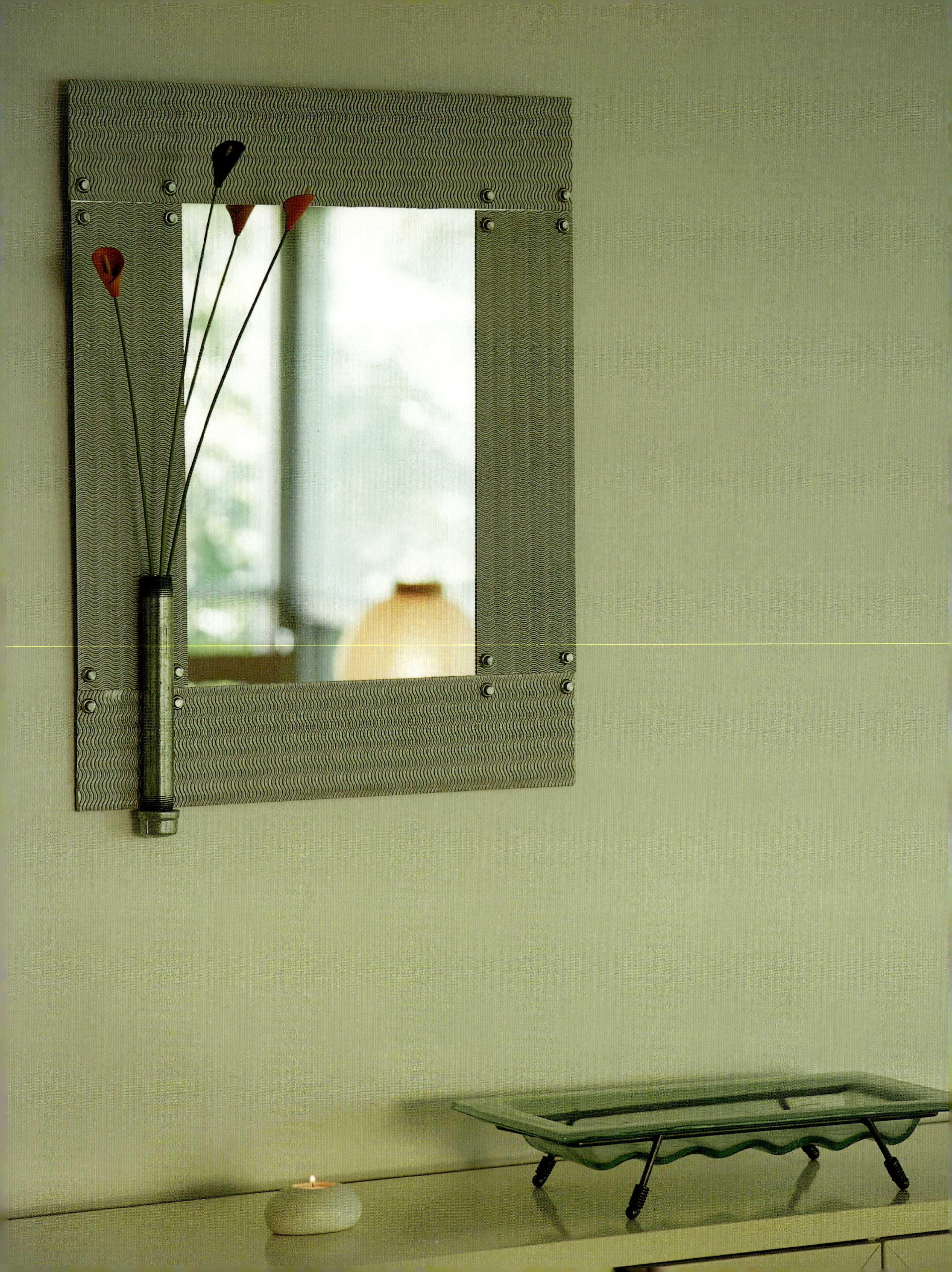

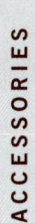

"metal"-framed mirror with vase

ACCESSORIES

Sheet-metal decor makes me pant like a puppy, but only those with hard-core tools are allowed to play. I don't have a plasma cutter, do you? We can faux it up, though, with embossed metallic paper and rudimentary hardware. And what better complement to a hunk of metal than delicate silk flowers?

24 x 30-inch mirror	Rubber gloves
Glass cleaner	Quick-drying two-part epoxy for glass and metal
Paper towels	
1 x 10-inch galvanized pipe nipple	2 disposable plates
1-inch galvanized end cap	2 craft sticks
Baking soda	Sixteen $5/16$-inch wood plugs
Sponge	Metallic silver spray paint
Long ruler	16 no. 2 zinc finishing washers
Craft knife	Marker
Self-healing cutting mat	Hot glue gun with glue sticks
Embossed metallic paper, at least 20 x 24 inches	2 ring hangers
	Picture wire
Pencil	Heavy-duty picture hanger with nail
Newspaper	Hammer
Decoupage medium	Silk flowers
Foam paintbrush	

1. Wipe the mirror with glass cleaner. Clean the pipe nipple and end cap with water, baking soda, and the sponge. Dry them off.

2. With the ruler, craft knife, and cutting mat, cut two 5 x 24-inch and two 5 x 20-inch strips from the paper. Arrange the strips as shown in the photograph, all edges lining up.

3. Place the mirror so that one of its short edges is hanging off your worktable. Put the end cap on the pipe nipple to make the vase and place it in the bottom left corner of the frame with the top of its cap butting the edge of the mirror. Hold down the vase and use the pencil to trace around its underside on the paper. Remove the vase and cut out the channel you marked.

4. Spread out some newspaper. One at a time, brush the backs of the paper with decoupage medium and press them in place on the mirror. Gently rub down all areas, taking care not to crush the embossing.

5. Wearing the rubber gloves, dispense equal parts of the epoxy onto a disposable plate and mix it together with a craft stick. Put epoxy on the channel you made for the vase, then press the vase onto the epoxy. Follow the epoxy manufacturer's instructions for cleaning up any glue that oozes onto the paper. Discard the plate and craft stick. Let the epoxy cure for the recommended time before moving the mirror.

6. Working outdoors or in a well-ventilated area, put down some newspaper and place the wood plugs with their wider sides up. Spray them silver. While they dry, put four washers near each paper seam as in the photo. Line them up evenly, then mark a dot in the center of each. Remove them one at a time, place hot glue on their undersides, and replace them over the dots. Hot glue a silver wood plug in the center of each.

7. Mix up another batch of epoxy and attach the two ring hangers to the mirror's backside. Once dry, wrap picture wire around each hanger, nail the heavy-duty hanger into the wall, and hang the mirror. Drop the flowers into the vase.

RETRO FRIDGE MAGNETS

If your magnetic poetry needs company, make your own refrigerator ornaments using stickers and cardboard. Place a round sticker on one color of card stock, cut a skewed rectangle around it, then glue that card on a larger card stock rectangle in a different color and skewed at a different angle. Attach an adhesive-coated magnet to the back.

minute mod 7

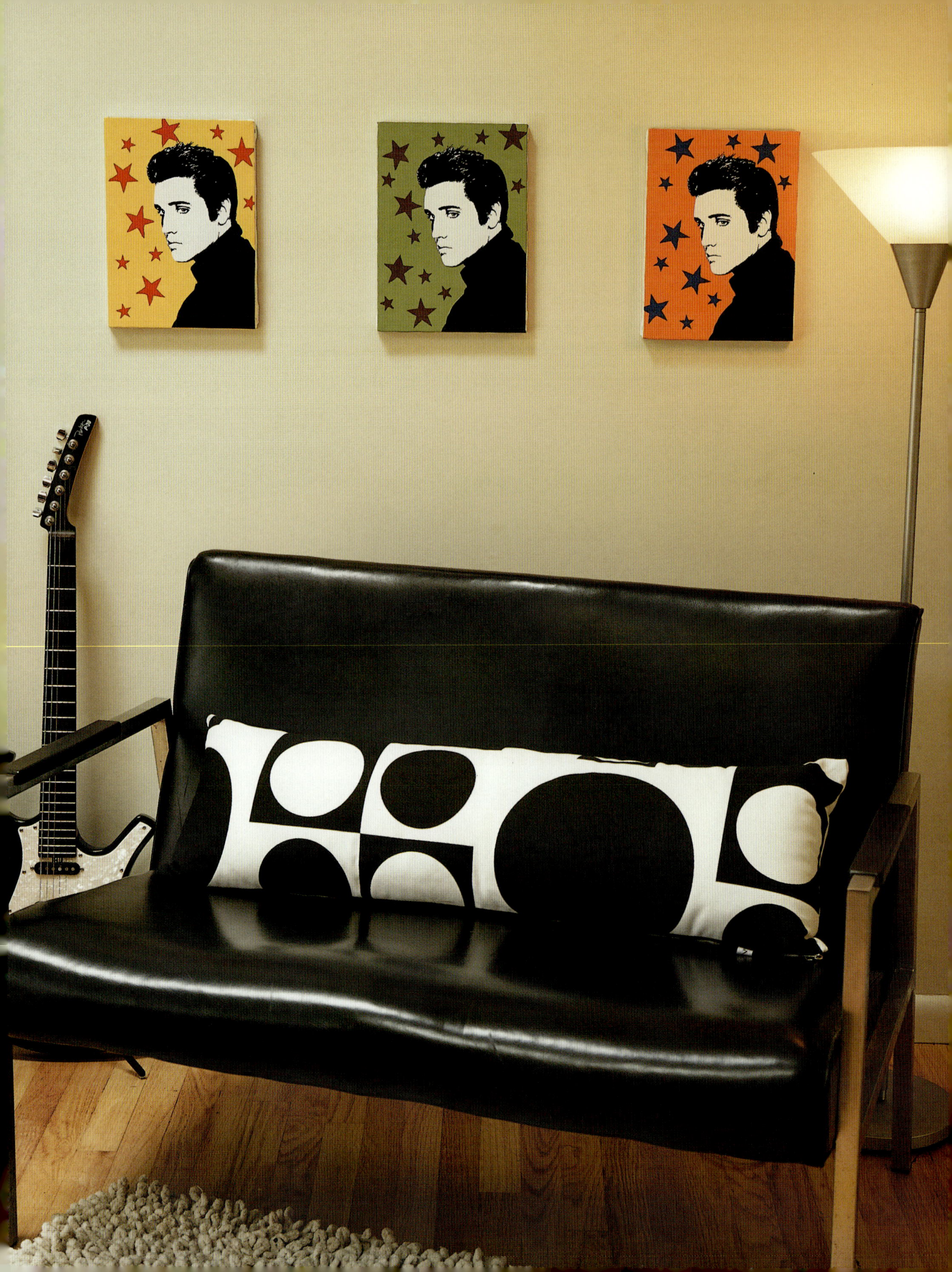

ART

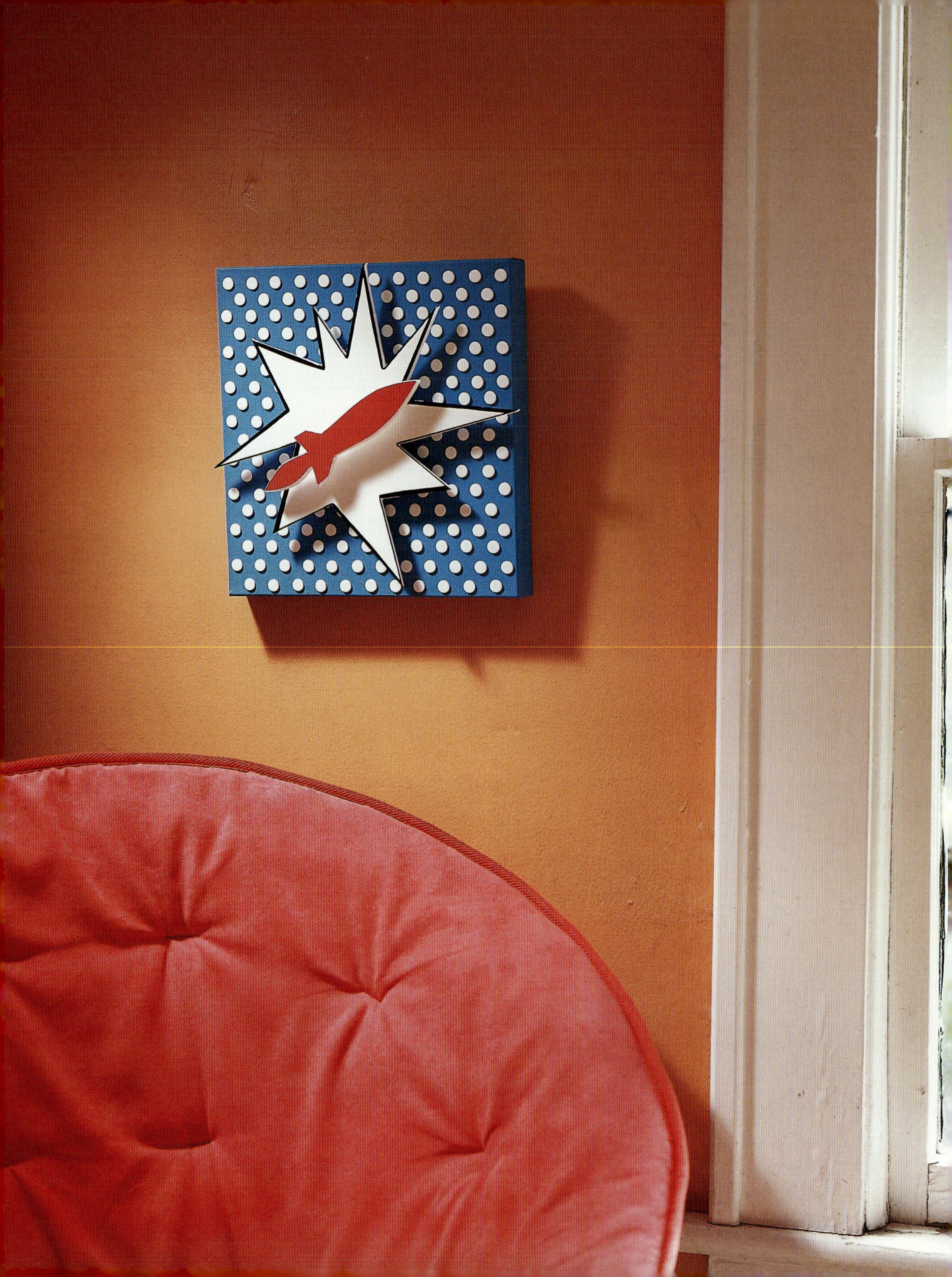

ART

3-D pop rocket

This comic book–inspired painting literally pops off the wall. The three-dimensional foam elements, propped up on adhesive dots made for scrapbooking, add an in-your-face quality that will recall the battling superheroes of your youth and the melodramatic paintings of Roy Lichtenstein. If the red rocket doesn't fire you up, individualize your painting with a different motif filched from clip art—try a fist, a bomb, or the word POW!

Bright blue acrylic paint
Foam paintbrush
12-inch square canvas with staple-free edges
Explosion and rocket templates
Scissors
Pencil
1 piece each white and red 1/4-inch-thick foam boards
12-inch ruler

Utility knife
Self-healing cutting mat
Black paint marker
200 adhesive foam dots, 1/16 inch thick and 1/2 inch wide (such as Pop Dots)

Enlarge and trace these templates.

ART

1. Paint the front and sides of the canvas blue. Let the paint dry, then apply a second coat.

2. On a copier, enlarge the explosion and rocket templates. Cut them out. Use the pencil to trace around the explosion on the white foam board, and the rocket on the red board. Cut them out using the ruler, utility knife, and mat. Outline the edges of the explosion with the paint marker.

3. In a few places on the back of the explosion, stack four adhesive dots on top of each other. Center the explosion over the canvas and press it down. In a couple places on the back of the rocket, stack four adhesive dots and press the rocket in the center of the explosion.

4. Put the ruler near the top edge of the canvas. Make a pencil mark at ½ inch, 1½ inches, 2½ inches, and so on until you've made 12 marks. Center an adhesive dot over each mark. Do not peel off the paper covering the adhesive on the side of the dots that faces up. Put the ruler below this row of dots and make marks at 1 inch, 2 inches, 3 inches, and so on until you've made 11 marks. Put adhesive dots over these marks. Alternate the 12- and 11-dot rows until you have covered the visible part of the canvas. Work around the explosion.

trace-and-cut collage

ART

In a pinch for a dash of color, you may have stretched fabric over a canvas and called it instant art. This project goes a step further by translating a textile's pattern into paper cutouts, introducing texture and a hand-crafted quality. A kindergartner could master the simple process: you'll make the collage with scissors (plastic safety type optional), paper, and paste. The hand-cut frame is balsa, the featherweight wood of model airplanes, and requires no expensive glass or mat.

Long ruler
Utility knife
Self-healing cutting mat
20 x 30 x $1/2$-inch white foam board
Pencil
At least $1/2$ yard fabric with a pattern you want to trace
Scissors
Drawing papers in the colors of your fabric
Graphite tracing paper
Stylus tool, such as pen with a pointed cap
Foam paintbrush

Matte decoupage medium
8 feet of 3 x $1/16$-inch balsa wood (available in the woodworking section of craft stores; you may have to buy four 36-inch-long strips, which will result in leftover wood)
Protractor
Newspaper
Rubber gloves
Satin polyurethane
Cotton rag
Tape
Adhesive mounting squares

1. With the ruler, utility knife, and mat, cut down the foam board to 20 x 25 inches. Use the pencil and ruler to draw a $2^{1}/_{2}$-inch border all around it.

2. Cut a 15 x 20-inch rectangle from the fabric to be your collage's template. To trace the fabric's shapes, place the tracing paper, graphite side down, on top of a piece of colored drawing paper. Place the fabric on top of the tracing paper and use the stylus to trace the shapes that match the color of the drawing paper you're currently working with. Repeat the tracing for each color of paper.

ART

3. When you're ready to glue paper shapes onto the foam board, it's best to start in a corner and work your way out. Cut out one shape at a time, just inside the graphite lines. Brush the back of it with decoupage medium and set it on the foam board inside the marked border. Cut out the next shape, glue it down, and so on.

4. When the glue is dry, brush a coat of decoupage medium over the entire surface of the collage. Let the glue dry, then apply a second coat.

5. Mark the balsa wood for cuts: two lengths at 20 inches and two at 15 inches. Since these will be the inner edges of the frame and you will be making 45-degree miter cuts that angle away from your marks, the outer edges of the frame will be longer. Take care to leave adequate space around your marks to accommodate the cuts. Use the protractor to mark the angles, then make the cuts with the utility knife, ruler, and mat.

6. Place the balsa pieces around the collage to ensure that they fit together. Make adjustments if necessary. Take the wood outdoors or to a well-ventilated area, cover your work surface with newspaper, and put on the gloves. Apply polyurethane to the front of each balsa piece with the rag. Let it dry, then apply a second coat.

7. When the wood is dry, flip the pieces polyurethane-side-down, line up the mitered corners, and tape the edges where they meet. Drizzle decoupage medium in the border area of the foam board, then press the frame, taped-side-down, onto the collage. Put mounting squares on the back and hang.

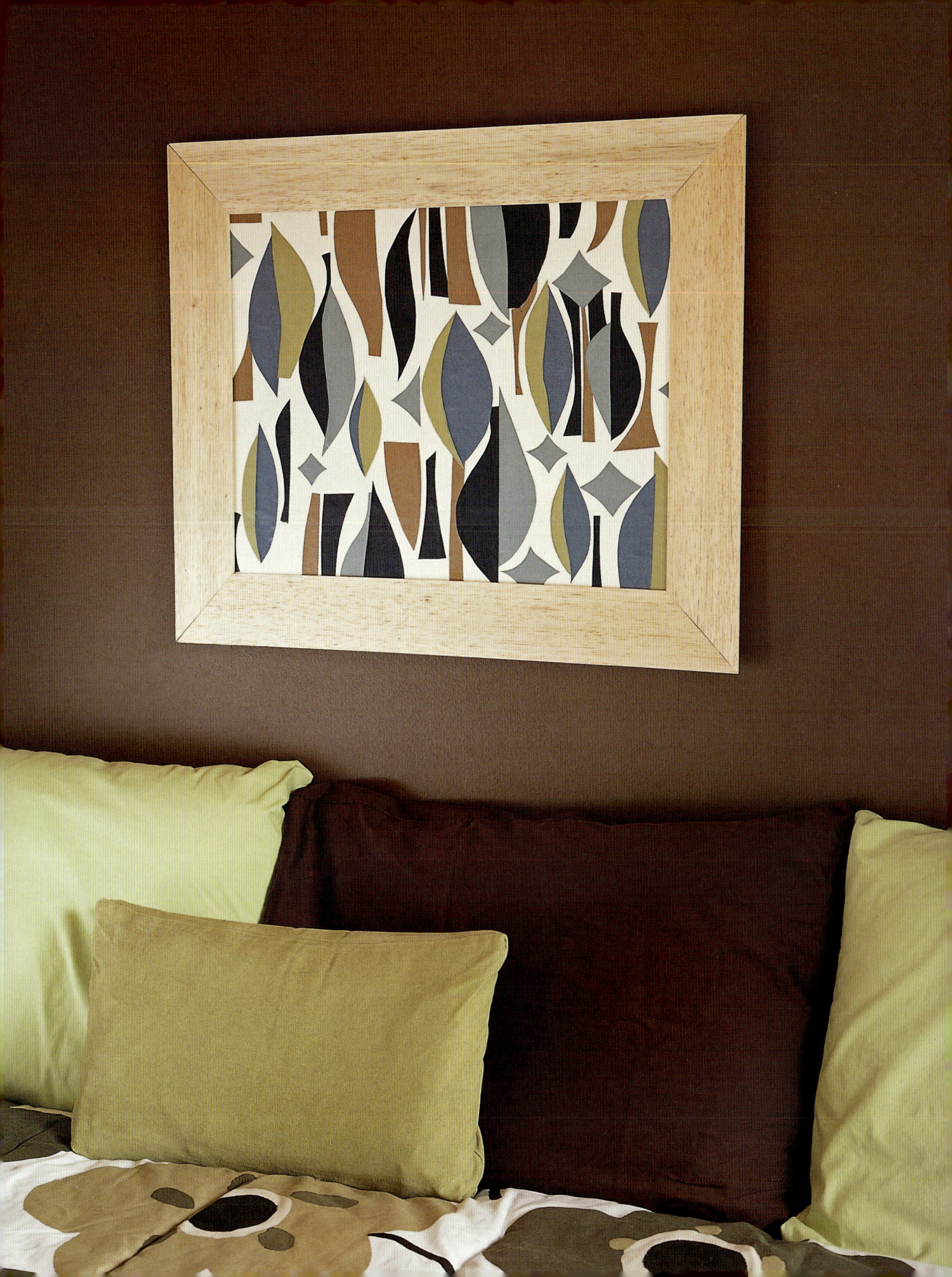

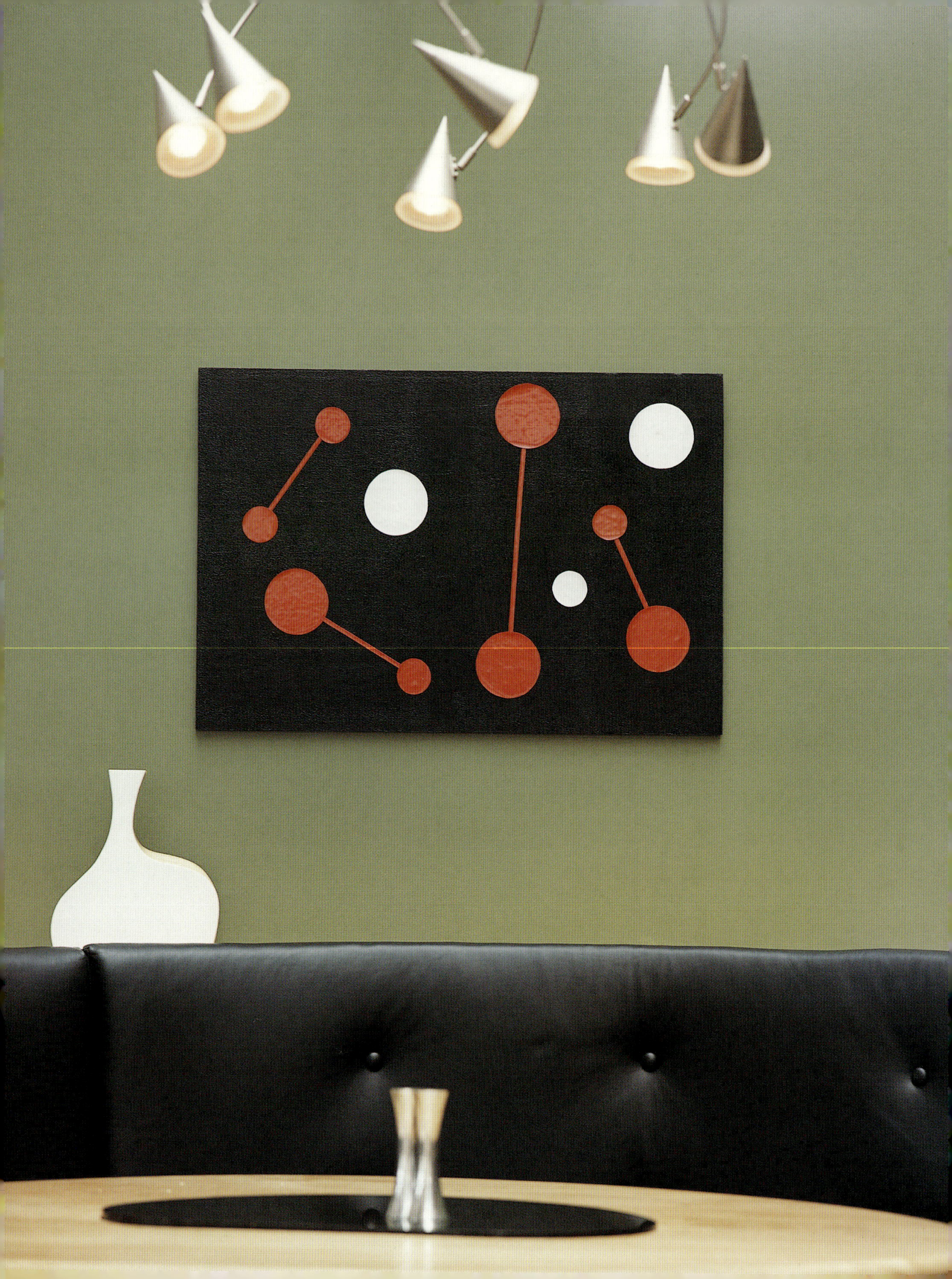

movable magnetic art

ART

Interactive exhibits aren't just for children's museums. Magnetic paint and printable magnetic sheets make for an abstract creation that can evolve daily. Friends love to move the magnets when they're visiting; you can even make several small versions as conversation starters for your next party. And when you're tired of one composition, just print more magnet sheets in different colors and cut out new shapes.

2 mini foam rollers
2 small paint trays
1 pint magnetic paint
20 x 30 x $1/2$-inch foam board
1 pint flat black latex paint
Three $8 1/2$ x 11-inch printable magnetic sheets
Ruler
Craft knife
Self-healing cutting mat
Circular objects in two sizes, such as a drinking glass and a shot glass
Pencil
Scissors
Adhesive mounting squares

1. Using a roller and tray, apply a coat of magnetic paint, as smoothly as possible, to the foam board. Let it dry, then apply a second coat. When the paint is dry, test its magnetic strength using a magnetic sheet. If the hold is not good, apply a third coat. Discard the used roller and tray.

2. Apply one or more coats of black paint to the magnetic board.

3. On a computer, draw a box that fills the page and color it red. Print the red box onto two of the magnetic sheets. Leave the third magnetic sheet white.

4. With the ruler, craft knife, and mat, cut $1/4$-inch strips of the red sheets in different lengths. To make the circles, on the unprinted side of the magnets, trace around the glasses with a pencil, then cut out the circles with scissors. Make both red and white circles.

ART

5. Put your magnetic pieces on the board. Connect red circles with red slices to make dumbbell shapes. Place white circles around randomly.

6. Put mounting squares on the back and hang. Change the art whenever you like.

The special iron-laden magnetic paint is heavy, so use a thick foam board that won't warp. You could also use a sturdy canvas.

ART

celebrity triptych

Who says you need skills to be a portrait artist? Many Web sites offer royalty-free celebrity photographs that you can copy and incorporate into art. Use stamped shapes and a solid background in complementary colors for a Warhol-like look. Voilà! A vibrant triple tribute to your favorite star.

Digital royalty-free celebrity photograph
8½ x 11-inch matte photo paper
Scissors
Three 9 x 12-inch canvases
Acrylic paints in yellow, green, orange, red, purple, and blue
Foam paintbrushes
Decoupage medium
Artist's brushes
Star-shaped foam stamps in two sizes

1. Open the digital file in a photo program and make the picture black and white, if it's not already. Adjust the contrast to 100 percent, which basically turns the photo into line art—no gray.

2. Size the image so that it will fill out about three-quarters of your paper. Print out three copies on the matte photo paper. Cut out the images and set them aside.

3. Paint the three canvases yellow, green, and orange and let them dry. Paint second coats, if necessary, and let them dry.

4. Brush the back of one cutout with decoupage medium, making sure to coat all edges and stray pieces, such as hair. Smooth down the cutout onto a painted canvas. Repeat with the other two.

ART

5. Use the artist's brushes to paint complementary colors onto the star stamps (red with yellow, purple with green, blue with orange). Stamp the two sizes in a random pattern around your celebrity. Touch up areas with the brushes. Wash and dry the stamps when you change colors.

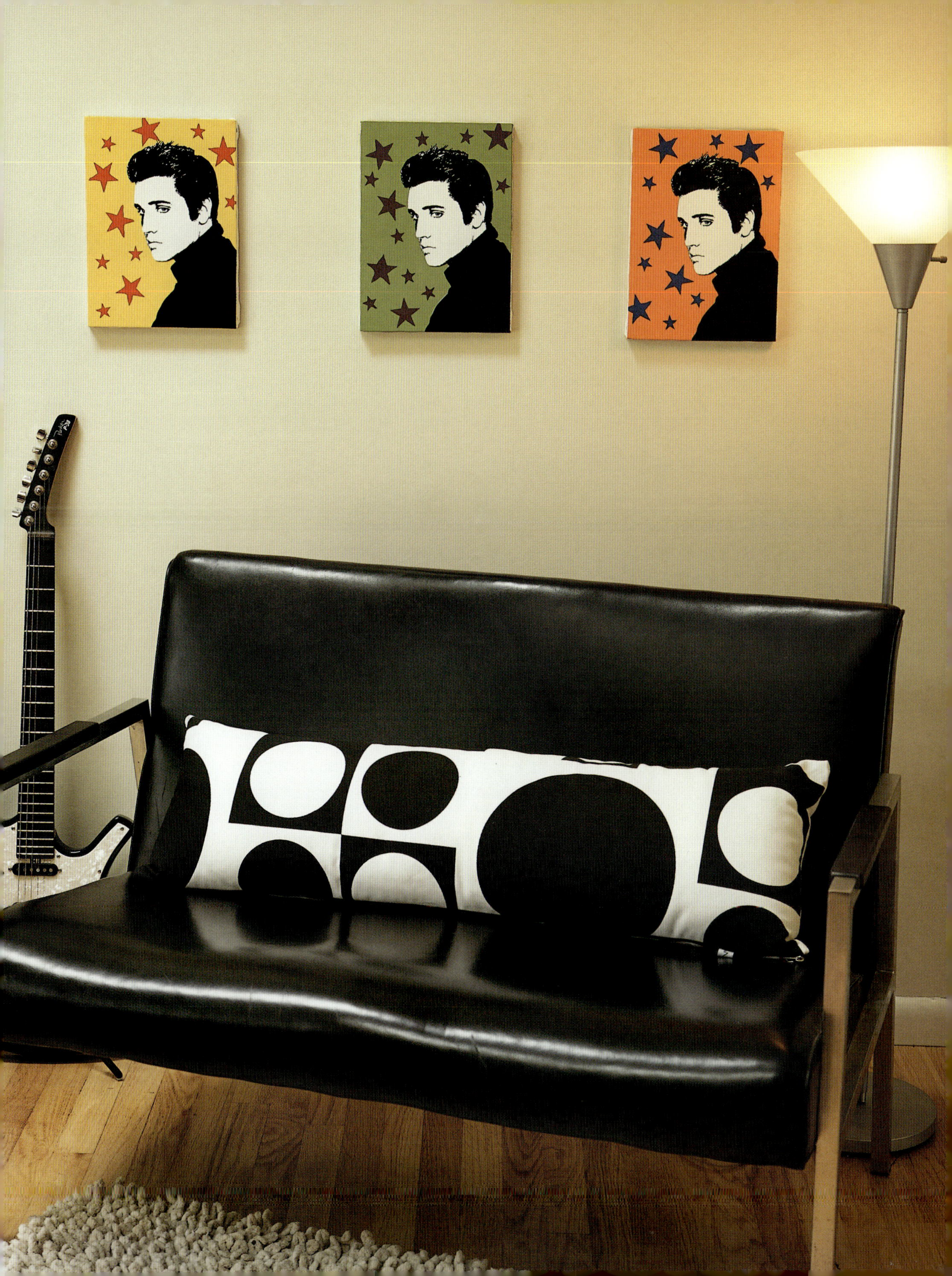

soup label assembly

ART

Repetition—even of the most banal supermarket item—is beauty, as Andy Warhol demonstrated. Stock up on soup or other canned goods with pleasing labels and assemble a simple collage in minutes. Before you can say "add water, heat, and serve," your artwork will be ready to hang. Just be sure to label your naked cans with a permanent marker so that your next lunch isn't a mystery.

Craft knife
16 same-size canned goods
Ruler
Pencil

Self-healing cutting mat
Cellophane tape
Frame with an 11 x 14-inch mat

1. Use the craft knife to strip the labels off the cans.

2. Use the ruler and pencil to mark a $2^{3}/_{4}$ x $3^{1}/_{2}$-inch rectangle on each label, centered around the graphics. Trim the labels with the craft knife and cutting mat, then arrange them randomly in four rows of four.

3. Turn the labels over and tape their edges together. Periodically turn the assembly right side up to make sure the graphics are aligned. Carefully lift the tape and adjust the labels if necessary.

4. Place the assembled labels inside the frame and hang.

Campbell's Chicken Noodle Soup
Campbell's Tomato Soup
Campbell's Chicken Noodle Soup
Campbell's Cream of Mushroom Soup
Campbell's Chicken Noodle Soup
Campbell's Tomato Soup
Campbell's Tomato Soup
Campbell's Cream of Mushroom Soup
Campbell's Cream of Mushroom Soup
Campbell's Tomato Soup
Campbell's Cream of Mushroom Soup
Campbell's Tomato Soup
Campbell's Tomato
Campbell's Chicken Noodle
Campbell's Chicken Noodle
Campbell's Cream of Mushroom

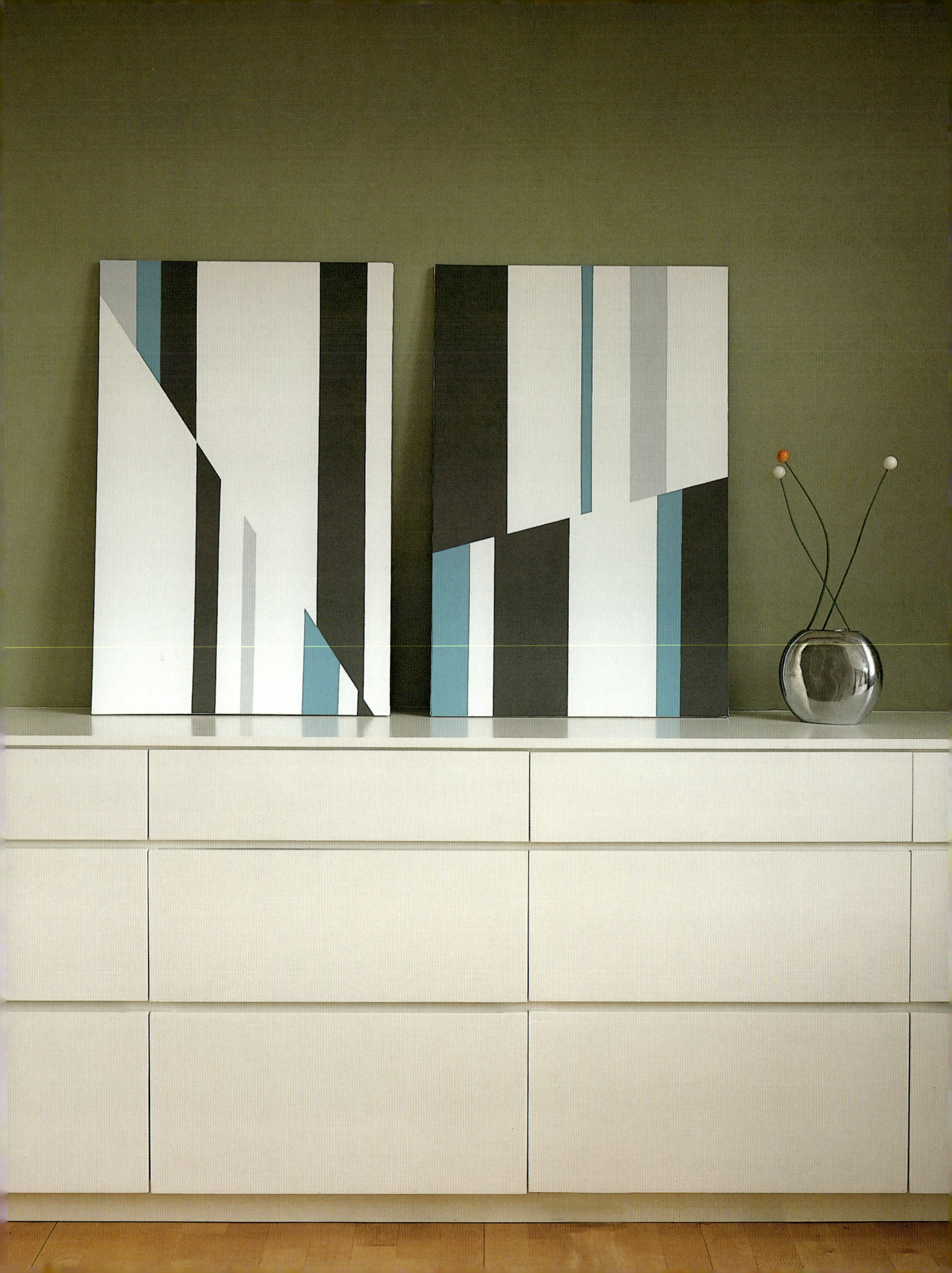

masked stripes paintings

ART

While browsing a contemporary gallery with prices in the quadruple digits, ever snidely mumble to your bud, "That looks so easy! Even I could paint that"? Here's your chance to put your masking tape where your mouth is. These boldly striped canvases come together in stages; you need patience but no skills.

Wide masking tape
Two 24 x 36-inch canvases
L-shaped ruler
Pencil
Narrow masking tape
Acrylic paints in light gray, dark gray, and turquoise
Wide and narrow foam paintbrushes

1. Place a piece of wide masking tape diagonally across each canvas and rub down the edges of the tape. You will work on one side of this diagonal line at a time. Along one of the short edges of each canvas (not on the canvas face), measure and mark lines for the widths of the stripes in that half of the painting (see figure 14). Write the initial of the color that will go in each section.

2. Use the L-shaped ruler and pencil to mark the widths of the stripes on the diagonal tape as well so you can make parallel lines. Connect your marks on the canvas edge and diagonal tape with narrow tape to create the masks for the stripes. (Note that where two colors [nonwhite] butt, you can mask and paint only one at a time. Mask and paint left-out stripes after their neighbors are dry.)

3. Paint the stripes. Let them dry and paint a second coat, if necessary.

4. After all the stripes are dry, remove the vertical tape. Move the diagonal tape to the painted side of the line. Mark, tape, and paint the stripes on the unpainted halves of the canvases as above. Remove the tape.

Figure 14

G = gray
D = dark gray
T = turquoise
W = white (no paint)
All numbers in inches

172

GIFT BOX ART

After a present-exchanging fête, gather up small gift boxes and tissue paper scraps and make these mini collages. The tops and bottoms of rigid two-piece boxes used for jewelry work best. Cut out shapes from the tissue using a rotary cutter, self-healing mat, and ruler; gently rub the tissue pieces with a glue stick (not a wet glue); and smooth them onto the boxes. Hang your petite artwork on small nails angled upward.

minute mod

index

Accessories, 31–33
    Household Icons, 137–38
    "Metal"-Framed Mirror with Vase, 151–52
    Mostly No-Sew Pillows, 147–49
    Plastic Mesh Coasters, 144–45
    Recycled Drink Markers, 111
    Retro Fridge Magnets, 153
    Spray-Painted Bud Vases, 143
    Sunny Atomic Clock, 139–41
Adjustable Globe Ceiling Fixture, 74–77
Amoeba Box Light, 71–73
Arranging furnishings, 29, 30–31
Art
    Celebrity Triptych, 165–67
    Gift Box Art, 173
    Mask Stripes Paintings, 171–72
    Movable Magnetic Art, 163–64
    Soup Label Assembly, 168–69
    3-D Pop Rocket, 157–58
    Trace-and-Cut Collage, 159–61
Art Paper Tube Shade, 61–63
Blueprint Sconce, 79–81
Canvas Folding Screen, 104–6
Card Stock Wall Grid, 115–16
Celebrity Triptych, 165–67
Clip-Art Café Curtain, 43–44
Colors, 24–26
Decoupaged Dresser, 85–86

Domino Backsplash, 117–19
Drink markers, recycled, 111
Fabric, harmonizing, 20, 21–24
Fabric-Covered Roller Shade, 49
Fabric-Striped Wall, 119–22
Faux Leopard Rug, 129, 130
Floors
    Faux Leopard Rug, 129, 130
    Inlaid Faux Fur Rug, 131–33
    Painted Floorcloth, 127–28
Furniture
    arranging, 29, 30–31
    Canvas Folding Screen, 104–6
    choosing, 26–28
    Decoupaged Dresser, 85–86
    Low Sling Chair, 95–96
    Pizza Pan Pedestal, 91–93
    quality/economy, 27–28
    Rolling Two-Tier Coffee Table, 97–99
    Slipcovered Crate Ottoman, 101–3
    transforming office chairs, 25
    Woven Vinyl Headboard, 89–90
    "Zebrawood" Bedside Tables, 107–10
Gift Box Art, 173
Harmony, 21–24
Household Icons, 137–38
Inlaid Faux Fur Rug, 131–33
Lightbulb Curtain Finials, 53–55

Lighting
    Adjustable Globe Ceiling Fixture, 74–77
    Amoeba Box Light, 71–73
    Art Paper Tube Shade, 61–63
    Blueprint Sconce, 79–81
    Plastic Mosaic Lamp Shade, 59–60
    Stacked Shade Lantern, 65–67
    Toilet-Inspired Torchère, 69–70
Low Sling Chair, 95–96
Mask Stripes Paintings, 171–72
Memo Pad Mosaic Border, 123–25
"Metal"-Framed Mirror with Vase, 151–52
Mondrian "Stained-Glass" Window, 51–52
Movable Magnetic Art, 163–64
Office chairs, transforming, 25
Painted Floorcloth, 127–28
Pillows, 147–49
Pizza Pan Pedestal, 91–93
Planning
    colors, 24–26
    creating harmony and, 21–24
    harmony and, 21–24
    scoping room and, 19–20
    themes, 17–18
Plastic Mesh Coasters, 144–45
Plastic Mosaic Lamp Shade, 59–60
Polka-Dot Appliqué Panels, 37–38
Recycled Drink Markers, 111
Retro fabric, 87
Retro Fridge Magnets, 153
Rolling Two-Tier Coffee Table, 97–99
Scoping room, 19–20
Slipcovered Crate Ottoman, 101–3
Soup Label Assembly, 168–69
Spray-Painted Bud Vases, 143
Stacked Shade Lantern, 65–67
Studded Plum Sheer, 39–41
Sunny Atomic Clock, 139–41
Themes, 17–18
3-D Pop Rocket, 157–58
Toilet-Inspired Torchère, 69–70
Upholstered Cardboard Valance, 45–47
Walls
    Card Stock Wall Grid, 115–16
    Domino Backsplash, 117–19
    Fabric-Striped Wall, 119–22
    Memo Pad Mosaic Border, 123–25
White walls, 22
Window treatments
    Clip-Art Café Curtain, 43–44
    Fabric-Covered Roller Shade, 49
    Lightbulb Curtain Finials, 53–55
    Mondrian "Stained-Glass" Window, 51–52
    Polka-Dot Appliqué Panels, 37–38
    Studded Plum Sheer, 39–41
    Upholstered Cardboard Valance, 45–47
Woven Vinyl Headboard, 89–90
"Zebrawood" Bedside Tables, 107–10

about the author

Jeanée Ledoux owns the successful freelance business Afterword Editorial Services in Decatur, Georgia. By day she copyedits and proofreads nonfiction; by night she gets crafty and writes DIY articles for newspapers and magazines. Her passion is creating with her hands, from home decor to jewelry to meals. She lives and decorates with her photographer husband, Andrea, and their furry friends Leroy, Moonpie, and Lucy.